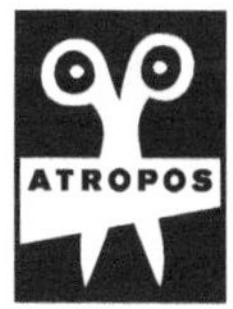

ATROPOS PRESS
new york • dresden

Think Media EGS Series is supported by the European Graduate School

ATROPOS PRESS
New York • Dresden

151 First Avenue # 14, New York, N.Y. 10003

cover design: Peggy Bloomer

ISBN 978-1-940813-22-6

Creative Deactualization: Rethinking the Idea of Revolution

By Chahid Akoury

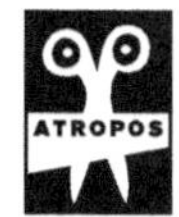

ATROPOS PRESS
new york • dresden

Acknowledgments

I thank my advisor Herr Professor Doktor Wolfgang Schirmacher for making the Idea of a creative gathering possible in the European Graduate School, a site for conversations that spur all that is intellectually new.

I am grateful to Slavoj Žižek for giving me some of his time, and for discussing with me the various approaches I had throughout my brainstorming process and my initial formulation of my thesis; be it through the conversations we had around meals at the Hotel Allalin, during class discussions, or in replying to my e-mails.

I am forever grateful to my amazing wife for her unconditional support and understanding. I owe this dissertation to her sacrifices and motivation.

Furthermore, I extend my thanks to everyone who has influenced me over the years whether directly or indirectly.

Table of Contents

"Wie beginnt eine Veränderung, wie entsteht Neues? Muß das Ungewohnte bereits geschehen sein, bevor wir eine Veränderung überhaupt wahrnehmen? Oder haben wir zunächst zu erdenken, was dann zur Tat wird?"

—Wolfgang Schirmacher, *Die Stadt Als Geviert*

"A revolution is a return from the factitious to the real."

— Victor Hugo, *Les Miserables*

"The oppressed are allowed once every few years to decide which particular representatives of the oppressing class are to represent and repress them."

— Karl Marx

1. Introduction

Immanence and the Radically New

Over the past decade, there has been an emergence of worldwide movements as well as continuous riots, strikes, and occupations. One might characterize these mobilizations as struggling against emerging crises created by the structures of social political and economic organizations. The general rhetoric being that of change, however change has come to signify nothing more than a mere shift from one side to the other, substitution of political alternatives, rather than being a new stage of coherent development.

Change in its current approach is already a characteristic of our reality; it pervades the natural, the socio-economic, the political, the technological, and the cultural. As such our world is in a constant state of progress and invention. Nevertheless, if all change is immanent, then how does the new enter the world?

The imperative of change should be that of the life world itself, as a radical change, one that engages with reality and revolutionizes every single aspect of it, disrupting its structure, processes, and operation. It is only through the radical break, which excludes the world as we know it, that the new emerges.

Change Beyond the Specular Play with Reality

Wolfgang Schirmacher urges us to "admit that the conflicts we face are unresolvable, with the theoretical and practical means we have at our disposal, we are merely attempting to treat the symptoms: such an admission could well amount to a turning point."[1] Schirmacher continues:

> We must refuse to recognize problems as they are posed to us: objective necessities, justified interests, societal goals, assessment of consequences, codified or unwritten rights—all these conspire to relieve us of responsibility at the source. What is demanded of us instead is that we share the burdens and share in the solutions to problems whose emergence we had nothing to do with. "Guilt by association" is hardly a sufficient legitimation of the call for commitment and support. The miscarried and generally botched present-day world must face its problems on its own. The oft-maligned postmodern escapism is the justified refusal to reward, even by acknowledgement, the perpetrators for their deeds. But this does not mean that we are going to put up with the poisoning of our waters or the impoverishment of the Third World. On the contrary, our refusal to acknowledge prefabricated problems and help implement their supposedly realistic solutions is the very thing that enables us to generate our own world and to stake our entire existence on its emergence.[2]

Schirmacher asserts what we have been attempting to do as far as positing the problems and finding solutions for them, has played a major role in rendering us incapable of genuine change. Moreover, the first step out of this deadlock is by acknowledging the inefficiency of our approaches, since they elude the very condition of our predicament, where instead of succumbing to the representation of the problematic, we resist this world and its posed conflict towards true emancipation. Schirmacher proposes we refuse to acknowledge the endowed problems of our reality, and in doing so we are giving way to another world to emerge. Instead of being caught within the scope of solving whatever we are bombarded with as crises that emanate from our current condition, we should problematize this very condition, and it is only then that we are able to radically change in favor of another world.

In a discussion with Jean Francois Lyotard, Schirmacher affirms this change occurs to no transcendental extent, it is instead instigated by self-examination, which we as humans "always already" engage in under the form of self-evaluation. As Schirmacher asserts, one has to overcome restricting this self-evaluation to "personal circumstances, social and professional success, or one's own health"[3], in favor of an evaluation undertaken from within. As corollary to Schirmacher's proposed premise, my thesis refers to change from within, not as "a mere specular play with the contemporary world as it takes place",[4] rather as what is radically divergent.

Put differently, the aim of this project is to consider revolution not as an answer to a problem, but the problematic Idea itself. Rather than remaining caught in repeated patterns of true and false solutions to deal with the problem as if that is all there is or can be, this text will think "revolution" as the generator of the impossible, the radical otherness "to come", in opening up "free spaces of unregulation, which so loosen an arrangement as to allow for sensations of something new, other affects, other percepts."[5]

In this respect, radical change is inherent to the idea of revolution, and it is only through recognizing the significance of the Idea to spur the truly New, yet at the same time differentiating it, as Idea, from the attempts of its historical realizations.[6]

The Crisis of Change in the Contemporary Context: In Medias Res

"Revolutions are the only political events which confront us directly and inevitably with the problem of beginning."

— Hannah Arendt, *On Revolution*

Franco "Bifo" Berardi propounds the 2011 uprisings heralded a deep crisis, "one that seemed more a crisis of imagination than mere economics."[7] Berardi adds, "this is a crisis of imagination about the future."[8] Bifo belongs to the '68 generation, and as such advises us not to expect that current uprisings hold any restoration of democracy in "the return of social solidarity and the reversal of the current financial dictatorship. We should be able to enhance the space of our historical prefiguration, so as to become able to abandon the conceptual framework of historical progress, and to imagine the prospect of irreversibility."[9] We are dead in the middle of things, and all the riots, uprisings and mobilizations start right in the action, as if revolts and mobilizations pick up where their precedents have left. The drawback resides not only in repeating the outworn structure of past revolution, which are subject to different contingencies and conditions, but in assuming that the conflict is expected to redeem that which the past moment failed to accomplish. It is a cyclical repetition of the same over and over around a fixed center, a blank revolution if there ever was one, with no purpose. Instead of opening up for the future to come, or learning from the mistakes of the past, this revolution is caught in the middle.

It is time to resist approaching any current or future emancipatory act as a continuity of what revolution stood for in the past:

> Although sublime moments like the Jacobin climax of the French Revolution and the October Revolution will forever remain a key part of our memory, the general framework has to be surpassed, and everything should be re-thought, beginning from the zero-point.[10]

To begin from the beginning proves to be the only way out of this deadlock, since it is only then that we free the Idea of revolution from its historical representations, and by doing so we are able to rethink what we mean by revolution.

Ten years ago mobilizations and protest movements followed a nomadic approach. They went wherever global institutions and organizations met, from the World Trade Organization to the International Monetary Fund, the World Bank, and the G8 summits. In contrast, the current wave of insurrection occupies public spaces, and instead of moving around, they are grounded, refusing to move. "Their immobility is partly due to the fact that they are so deeply rooted in local and national social issues."[11]

During the 2009 edition of the Venice Biennale, The Argentinean Artist Tomás Saraceno presented *Galaxies Forming along Filaments, Like Droplets along the Strands of a Spider's Web*. The piece, which is made entirely of mounted elastic connectors in spherical web-like structures, occupied an entire room at the exhibition. Bruno Latour "would have loved to see, when the exhibition was dismantled, how quickly the spherical patterns would have collapsed once a few of their outside links had been severed." [12] Latour analogizes this collapse to all the mobilization groups protesting for a "solid identity that would resist globalization"[13], since the search for identity "inside" is directly linked to the quality of the "outside" connection—"as if being local and having an identity could possibly be severed from alterity and connection."[14]

Latour's analogy is evident in the aftermath of the global protests and occupy movements. Once the dictatorship is "toppled", or the financial crisis is "bailed out", soon enough what started off as the promise of emancipation towards the radically new, dissipates. One of the slogans of Occupy Wall Street was "I lost my job, but found an occupation"[15], the question however is, once the occupation is lost, and it is bound to lose, what next?

Posing the Question of Change

In Douglas Adam's *The Hitchhiker's Guide to the Universe*, a race of hyperintelligent beings decide to find out the answer to life, the universe, and everything. In order to do so, they commissioned the construction of a huge computer. Two programmers, Lunkwill and Fook, were charged with the task of turning on the computer and asking it for the answer. The computer, which is appropriately named Deep Thought, informs the programmers that it would require seven and a half million years to answer:

> "Seven and a half million years...!" they cried in chorus.
> "Yes," declaimed Deep Thought, "I said I'd have to think about it, didn't I?"
> [Seven and a half million years later.... Fook and Lunkwill are long gone, but their ancestors continue what they started]
> "We are the ones who will hear,"said Phouchg, "the answer to the great question of Life....The Universe...And Everything...!"
> "Shhh," said Loonquawl with a slight gesture. "I think Deep Thought is preparing to speak!"
> There was a moment's expectant pause while panels slowly came to life on the front of the console. Lights flashed on and off experimentally and settled down into a businesslike pattern. A soft low hum came from the communication channel.
> "Good Morning," said Deep Thought at last.
> "Er..good morning, O Deep Thought" said Loonquawl nervously, "do you have...er, that is..."
> "An Answer for you?" interrupted Deep Thought majestically. "Yes, I have."

> The two men shivered with expectancy. Their waiting had not been in vain.
> "There really is one?" breathed Phouchg.
> "There really is one," confirmed Deep Thought.
> "To Everything? To the great Question of Life, the Universe and everything?"
> "Yes."
> Both of the men had been trained for this moment, their lives had been a preparation for it, they had been selected at birth as those who would witness the answer, but even so they found themselves gasping and squirming like excited children.
> "And you're ready to give it to us?" urged Loonsuawl.
> "I am."
> "Now?"
> "Now," said Deep Thought.
> They both licked their dry lips.
> "Though I don't think," added Deep Thought. "that you're going to like it."
> "Doesn't matter!" said Phouchg. "We must know it! Now!"
> "Now?" inquired Deep Thought.
> "Yes! Now..."
> "All right," said the computer, and settled into silence again. The two men fidgeted. The tension was unbearable.
> "You're really not going to like it," observed Deep Thought.
> "Tell us!"
> "All right," said Deep Thought. "The Answer to the Great Question..."
> "Yes..!"
> "Of Life, the Universe and Everything..." said Deep Thought.
> "Yes...!"
> "Is..." said Deep Thought, and paused.
> "Yes...!"
> "Is..."
> "Yes...!!!...?"
> "Forty-two," said Deep Thought, with infinite majesty and calm."[16]

In our present predicament, we want answers to unemployment, our global financial crises, and our social and political unfreedom. And in this way, the answers we seem to receive are akin to that of Deep Thought, some absurd perplexing declaration. The worldwide multitudes that descended into the streets and occupied city squares have no program, future expectations, or plans. For Slavoj Žižek, "the situation is similar to psychoanalysis, where the patient knows the answer (his symptoms are such answers) but doesn't know to what they are answers, and the analyst has to formulate a question."[17]

As in *The Hitchhiker's Guide*, where the two men had been preparing for this moment of "revelation" their entire lives, so are the protestors, the dream of opposing the hegemonic has always been the driving force of the left. But acting in opposition to certain crises is not the answer, and it does not need a hyperintellingent computer, nor a visitor from the future to tell us that, but a recollection of the failed past attempts. We should resist looking for an answer, for it is the question that should drive us.

The aim of this project is to acknowledge the shortcomings of the current notion of revolution, and to rethink revolution as the genuine "openness and *clearing*, without which surprises and future developments remain impossible".[18]

At the core of my thesis is a Deleuzean reading of revolution. Deleuze is duly pertinent in order to read change as the being of becoming. Becoming corresponds to the notion of repetition: in the proper Deleuzean sense only through repetition that the new can emerge.

This means that repetition does not repeat what *effectively was* in the past, but the virtual vested in the past and dismissed in its past actualization. Put succinctly, through repetition we regain the creativity that was betrayed in the past actualization. Actualization is always a genuine creation, since it "breaks with resemblance as a process no less than it does with identity as a principle."[19] In this regard, my approach considers the idea of revolution without its historical "betrayals". Jean Baudrillard postulates "there are no longer any revolutions, in the contemporary world, there are now only convulsions. As in an allegedly perfect mechanism, a system that is too well integrated, there are no longer any crises, but malfunctions, faults, breakdowns, aneurysmal ruptures."[20] In order to reestablish revolution, we have to look for that which is in revolution but is not tethered to representation. For this very reason, I am not concerned with the historicity of revolution, nor is it my aim to position revolution as a repetition of the same universality but into different areas of struggle, for these are repetitions as representation. The task is to free the idea of revolution from mimesis, and reinstate it as an engagement whose outcome is uncertain.[21]

"Every revolutionary opinion draws part of its strength from a secret conviction that nothing can be changed."

— George Orwell, *Road to Wigan Pier*

"Without Revolutionary theory, there can be no Revolutionary Movement."

— Vladimir Lenin

2. The Deadlock of Revolution

Revolution as an Etymological Failure

The Etymology of the term "revolution" ineluctably presents us with a deadlock: it designates in the first place a circular temporal movement enacted by a self-repeating gesture around a fixed point, and alternately a break with the old oppressive structure, in opening up the possibility for something radically new to emerge.[22] Inherent to this problematic are the notions of repetition and difference; as a cyclical return to the old, revolution is an act of repetition, and in the rejection of the old towards the promise of the emergence of something new, it is one of difference.

Revolution: Noumenal or Phenomenal?

Nevertheless, if revolution is simultaneously leaving the past behind towards the emergence of what is radically new, and recurrence of past tropes and structures, then the idea of revolution is an idea of repeated failure. Perhaps one way to approach this is by discerning between what revolution is *in itself*, or the idea of revolution that posits it as *noumenon*, and revolution as *phenomenon*. In the strict Kantian notion of the term, what we come to perceive as revolution, as it happens in historical reality, is nothing but a representation of the idea of revolution, or to put in other words, revolution "as it is" (concept) may never correspond to how a revolution "appears to us". In his *Conflict of Faculties*, Kant arrives to the conclusion that even though change cannot be proven, we could nonetheless recognize signs indicating its possibility. Kant considers the French

Revolution to be that sort of a sign, as he writes:

> The recent Revolution of a people which is rich in spirit, may well either fail or succeed, accumulate misery and atrocity, it nevertheless arouses in the heart of all spectators (who are not themselves caught up in it) a taking of sides according to desires which borders on enthusiasm and which, since its very expression was not without danger, can only have been caused by a moral disposition within the human race.[23]

In Kant's opinion, what matters is not the revolution's content or its development as seen by those who make it, but merely its status as a *sign* or *spectacle* revealing the potential for "progress" in the Kantian sense. Conceptually, revolution as the Idea, although having no instantiations in the empirical world, must be thought as the promise of a radical break with the old, towards the opening up of something new. But as it happens, revolution presents itself as the return of the old. My inaugural intention here is to interrogate the idea of revolution in terms of the gap between thinking the revolution and doing it.

This Kantian enthusiasm, the hopes and dreams a revolutionary event instills in its viewers, could not be more evident than in our contemporary situation: riots, uprisings, and protests emerging almost everywhere around the world all demanding change. There seems to be a pressure to do something, to act as soon as possible, "Do it! Act first. Think later" says Jerry Rubin, "it is impulse not thinking that makes the great leaps forward. Theory comes when people try to figure out what they did *after* they do it."[24] Is this not evidently the dictum followed by all current revolutionary attempts, from the so-called Arab Spring[25] to the recent protests in Ankara?[26] But maybe it is time to take a step back think, and then do the right thing. As Slavoj Žižek suggests:

> True, we often talk about something instead of doing it; but sometimes we also do things in order to avoid talking and thinking about them…
>
> This emergence of an international protest movement, one without a program…reflects a deeper crisis…we have all the freedoms one

> wants: we feel free because we lack the very language to articulate our unfreedom...All the main terms we use to designate the present conflict – "war on terror", "democracy and freedom", "human rights", etc – are false terms, mystifying our perception of the situation instead of allowing us to think it.[27]

Žižek is proposing to think before we act.[28] Thinking our present situation through, in a radical manner, before impulsively acting out, or as Heidegger puts it "the most thought-provoking thing in our thought-provoking time is that we are still not thinking."[29] Is this not akin to Kant's proposition from *What is Enlightenment?* where the basic premise is that thinking, arguing, and criticizing will eventually pave the way for greater political and civil freedom? "A revolution may well bring about a falling off of personal despotism and of avaricious or tyrannical oppression, but never a true reform in one's way of thinking."[30] Kant's main concern here is that the new will simply replace the old in controlling the "great unthinking masses."[31] As a solution, he proposes to subtract thinking from acting, and it is only through this subtraction that a space opens up for the new to emerge. (Later, I will elaborate more on subtraction as opening up a space for the truly new, in Alain Badiou's sense of the term).

Let us shift our attention towards what T. J. Clark labels as "the first modernist painting", Jacques-Louis David's *The Death of Marat*.[32] What directly caught my attention, when I saw this painting for the first time, was the entirely obscure upper half of it, the black that seems to be the subject of the painting as much as the dying Marat is. I believe there are three ways which are relevant to my argument to read this painting. The first is in line with the previously discussed notion of subtraction, spacing as such, in David's case, the upper half is the unknown radical new the revolution is intended to bring forth (think of it as looking into Marat's final thoughts of what he believes the revolution to be). The second is as the gap, this "between" that such an opening brings forth—an obscure attempt to reconcile idea and experience. As for the third, I suggest it to be present in Vik Muniz's 2010 documentary *Waste Land.* Muniz recreates David's *The Death of Marat* with waste from the Jardim Gramacho landfill on the outskirts of Rio de Janeiro.[33] Muniz's reading, and in recreating the entire scene out of waste (the iconic representation of the

French Revolution, Jacques-Louis David's *The Death of Marat*) is invoking Walter Benjamin. For Benjamin, this might have been the motive of cultural history: to collect scraps and waste from the wreckage of culture, and reconstruct them, since we cannot understand history when we are engaged in things, only when these things are 'laid to waste' that we get it. We should not react to waste by trying to somehow get rid of it. Recalling yet another statement by Benjamin, one to do with visions from the future, as he writes in his *Arcades Project*, "the past has left images of itself in literary texts, images comparable to those which are imprinted by light on a photosensitive plate. The future alone possesses developers active enough to scan such surfaces perfectly."[34] In this precise sense is Muniz's recreation not a 'future development' of the original artwork? That idea of revolution as *noumenon* is literally *wasted* when you "Do It".[35] Thus, David deeply blackens the total upper half of the painting, be it as it were that the *phenomenon* or the experience of the revolution soiled (Did it!) the revolutionary idea.

And in line with Benjamin's future development, what we need is the moment of vision, *augenblick,* of reality, the waste land, since it is only then that we have a chance for rethinking the idea of revolution as such, the *public use of reason*, of suspending action, of thinking and as Žižek puts it, "without this moment of authentic passivity nothing New can emerge."[36]

So far, I have presented Kant's idea of revolution as a *noumenon* which cannot completely become a *phenomenon*, the revolution *in itself* is betrayed in its actualization. In other words, we face a situation in which revolution does not resemble its own idea, yet simultaneously this very idea is never fully justified in its representation of the revolutionary experience.

I will now turn to Gilles Deleuze who accounts for this problematic in his seminal work *Difference and Repetition*. Chapter five starts with Deleuze reading difference in terms of the Kantian Idea:

> Difference is not diversity. Diversity is given, but difference is that by which the given is given. Difference is not phenomenon, but the noumenon closest to the phenomenon.
>
> Every phenomenon refers to an inequality by which it is conditioned...Everything which happens and everything which appears

> is correlated with orders of differences: differences of level, temperature, pressure, tension, potential, difference of intensity. [37]

Although Deleuze resorts to Kant in addressing "things in themselves", difference *in itself* (pure difference) for Deleuze enables the possibility of an ontological happening, a becoming by which the given is given. This becoming is not a becoming of a being as an established entity, but as a process that establishes beings and transforms them. In this regard, revolution is not the rejection of every discipline, but the radical redefinition of what counts as discipline.

Hence, the Deleuzean *noumena* are not beyond human knowledge, as the Kantian approach asserts, but as Žižek explains they "are *even more phenomenal* than our shared phenomenal reality: they are the impossible phenomena, the phenomena excluded from our symbolically constituted reality,"[38] as intensive difference. And here, Žižek goes a step further to consider the idea of excessive intensity; those differences that are too intense as to explode a world from within. Therefore, it is in this case that we get to see things as they are "in themselves." And here I concur with the former point, in asserting that only through such excessive intensity that the revolution proper comes to be, anything less is a mere "anemic spectacle of life dragging on as its own shadow."[39] Following this very logic, is not the French revolution exactly this expression of intensive difference between the phenomenal and the noumenal? And in a Hegelian way, this very difference reverts into the phenomenal, as the schism between the normal revolutionary experience, and the impossible (*noumenon* closest to *phenomenon)*, the inhuman terror of the French revolution. Perhaps herein resides the Kantian nonchalance whether the revolution fails or succeeds, since what is pertinent is the emergence of difference, namely as the spectacle of the "internal explosive force"[40], the virtual intensities inherent in the *noumenon.*

Furthermore, Deleuze tells us repetition is not one of sameness, but one where pure difference emerges, i.e. only through repetition that intensive difference emerges—repetition that commits a difference in its very act. Is this notion of repetition not closely connected to the idea of revolution? And our challenge resides in making this idea clear, as the very driving force of radical change, in such a way as to break with the limits and conditions of possibility towards the production of difference. Put succinctly, instead of reducing the idea of revolution to its phenomenal by examining the conditions necessary for its appearance as *the thing in itself*, we should rethink the idea of revolution as "not yet the concept of an object which submits the world to the requirements of representation, but rather a brute presence which can be invoked in the world only in the function of that which is not representable in things."[41] In this sense, the following chapter rethinks the idea of revolution as repetition, as a kind of destabilization of reference, and as the presupposition for the possibility of change, following the point Deleuze makes that Idea (of revolution) should be freed from any attempts to relegate it into its representations, in order to bring forth proper difference. Furthermore, my reading will trace the idea of revolution as repetition, in three folds, starting with Hegel, followed by Marx, and ending with Deleuze's as the eternal return.

The approach I follow posits revolution in terms of the Deleuzean Idea, one that takes the notions of difference and repetition as its starting point, in the very sense of "a multiplicity of connections between differential relations embodied in real relations and actual terms".[42]

"Everything that needs to be said has already been said. But since no one was listening, everything must be said again."

— André Gide

"Progress, far from consisting in change, depends on retentiveness. When change is absolute there remains no being to improve and no direction is set for possible improvement: and when experience is not retained, as among savages, infancy is perpetual. Those who cannot remember the past are condemned to repeat it."

— Santayana, *Reason in Common Sense*

3. The Idea of Revolution

Revolution as Repetition with Difference

Hegel writes in the Philosophy of History: "By repetition, that which at first appeared merely a matter of chance and contingency becomes a real and ratified existence."[43]

What Hegel means is that repetition plays a vital role in history. "It is the passage from contingency to necessity."[44] When an event occurs once, it is dismissed as something that could have been avoided if one were to have dealt with the situation in a better way. However, if this same event is repeated, Hegel considers this as a sign of historical necessity. The revolution presents us with a choice, one in two stages. According to Hegel, the first choice has to be the wrong one, and it is only once we choose this wrong thing, that we are presented with the circumstances to make the right choice this time. First, it is the choice between the old, and a rupture from it. What this first choice does is that it renders or makes space for a repetition to begin anew, thus creating the condition for its emergence, in such a way that—and in referring to the French Revolution—"a 1794 is an inevitable and necessary corollary of each and every 1789".[45] "It is only after the radical negativity, the "terror" of abstract universality has done its work, can one choose between this abstract universality and concrete universality."[46] Only the "abstract" Terror of the French Revolution creates the conditions for the post-revolutionary "concrete" freedom. The following passage from Heinrich Heine's Paris Affairs perfectly illustrates the situation:

> When the intellectual developments or culture of a race are no longer in accord with its old established institutions, there results necessarily a combat in which the latter are overthrown; this is called a revolution. Until the revolution is complete, until that reformation of institutions does not perfectly agree with the intellectual development and the habits and wants of the people, just so long the national malady is not perfectly cured, and the sickly and excited people will often relapse into the weakness of exhaustion, yet ever and anon be subject to attacks or burning fever, when they tear away the tightest bandages and the most soothing lint from the old wounds, throw the most benevolent, noblest nurses out of the window, and roll about in agony until they finally find themselves in circumstances, that is, adapt themselves to institutions which suit them better.[47]

The revolutionary event has come to combat the outworn establishments of old. Rapid transformation of structures into new ones, in accordance with intellectual and cultural developments, is accompanied and carried through by violent events on the streets, events that are corollary, until finally we get to the right choice. What this means is that revolution is bound to the contingencies and circumstances of the situation it relates itself to, developments that lead to the disintegration of old institutions, until the rise of new suitable ones. Furthermore, the revolution is subject to necessity, in the sense that it posits itself as the radical break with the old.

Thus, revolution emerges as the repetition of the interaction between necessities and contingencies. However, this limited reading of revolution as repetition, posits it against the backdrop of *Aufhebung*, since there is no room in the Hegelian system for thinking pure repetition: the only Hegelian reading of repetition resides in the dialectical process, wherein a contingency is transformed to a necessity, and immediacy into universality. And in that sense, what the Hegelian dialectical process creates is a lack of the emergence of the New as repetition.

This is precisely the repetition this project refutes, a cyclical return to what the thing always already was. Slavoj Žižek accounts for this in *Less Than Nothing*, where he writes:

> Hegel does think repetition, but not a pure non-productive one, not a "mechanical" repetition which just strives for more of the

> same: his notion of repetition always involves sublation; in other words, through repetition, something is idealized, transformed from an immediate contingent reality to a notional universality (Caesar dies as a person and becomes a universal title); or, at least, through repetition, the necessity of an event is confirmed (Napoleon had to lose twice to get the message that his time was over, that his first defeat was not just an accident). The fact that Hegel misses the excess of purely mechanical repetition in no way implies that he is excessively focused on the New (the progress which takes place through idealizing *Aufhebung*)—on the contrary, bearing in mind that the radically New emerges only through pure repetition, we should say that Hegel's inability to think pure repetition is the obverse of his inability to think the radically New, that is, a New, which is not potentially already in the Old and has just to be brought out into the open through the work of dialectical deployment. [48]

As we have seen with Deleuze, "pure repetition"[49] is intimately connected to, and urges us to think of pure difference *in itself*, as multiplicity, whereas in Hegel one cannot account for the concept of difference *in itself*, as "pure multiplicity". The standard critique of Hegel is that his system is cyclical, in such a way which does not allow for the emergence of something new. Through the Hegelian dialectical process, things become what they always-already are, and as such it is a system of contradiction and identity.

An obvious critique of the Hegelian repetition as such, is found in Kierkegaard. But before I reproach Hegel by means of Kierkegaard, I will briefly explain Kierkegaard's notion of repetition using an incident that took place amidst the UK riots in 2011. For Kierkegaard, repetition signifies, not the closed circle of rememoration, but an unexpected unknown, as future revelation, which furnishes our cognitive and moral institutions. Repetition in this approach can either bring about something altogether new to emerge, or repeat the old, but in a new way.

M.C. Taylor, a North Carolina based musician, wrote and recorded songs that were supposed to be released as *Bad Debt*, his debut album under the *Hiss Golden Messenger* sobriquet.[50] Taylor's songs explored his personal anxieties, his notions of currency, debt, his place in this world, and his belief in God. However, the recordings never made it to the market, since the CD stock was destroyed during the London riots, when his distributor's warehouse was burned to the ground.

Taylor's first choice is contingent; it musically posits our contemporary issues of anxiety, currency, debt, and belonging to both state and religion. This choice was repeated, unwillingly, by the riots as expression of impotent rage and despair. The riots were precisely violent outbursts stemming from collective anxiety: "a consumerist desire violently redirected when unable to realize itself in the 'proper' way (by shopping). As such it presented itself as a kind of ironic reply to the consumerist ideology with which we are bombarded in our daily lives: You call on us to consume while simultaneously depriving us of the possibility to do it properly—so here we are doing it the only way open to us." [51]

In Hegelian terms, the consequences of the fire are the very same contingencies that Taylor's debut album hinges on, that is to say alienation, debt, and monetary and professional loss. In addition, the new here is not a radical new content, but another development of the first choice; what was contingent has become necessary, rendering the old in a new fashion, Taylor's expression of anxiety was repeated on a mass scale as the violent frenzy in the streets of London.

Nonetheless, Kierkegaard considers this repetition a complete failure, since any attempt to reconcile the thing as it were before the repetition leaves us feeling dismal. And this is precisely my starting premise.

Another point to be made, one that is 'beyond Hegel', is Marx's consideration of the problem of repetition as such. In the introduction to *The Eighteenth Brumaire of Louis Bonaparte*, Marx considers the Hegelian notion of repetition, and supplements it, stating that Hegel "forgot to add: the first time as tragedy, the second as farce."[52] Marx's consideration stems from his observation of how the tragic transformation of the French Revolution into the events that followed 1789, had established the contingencies for its own farcical repetition in 1848 as the "grotesquely mediocre"[53] Louis Bonaparte, in the role of its hero.

In this perspective, almost all of the current protests from the 2010 student riots to the recent Turkish riots and everything in between, appear as farce—violent outbursts escalating out of control, thus exceeding the reasonable.

And through Marx's supplement, we reach Deleuze who concurs

with this twice appearance of repetition; once tragic, and once comic. While using the theatre as a starting ground, he elaborates:

> Hegel substitutes the abstract relation of the particular to the concept in general for the true relation of the singular and the universal in the Idea.
> He thus remains in the reflected element of representation, within simple generality. He represents concepts instead of dramatizing Ideas: he creates a false theatre, a false drama, a false movement. We must see how Hegel betrays and distorts the immediate in order to ground his dialectic in that incomprehension, and to introduce mediation in a movement which is no more than that of his own thought and its generalities. When we say, on the contrary, that movement is repetition and that this is our true theatre, we are not speaking of the effort of the actor who 'repeats' because he has not yet learned the part. We have in mind the theatrical space, the emptiness of that space, and the manner in which it is filled and determined by the signs and masks through which the actor plays a role which plays other roles; we think of how repetition is woven from one distinctive point to another, including the differences within itself. (When Marx also criticizes the abstract false movement or mediation of the Hegelians, he finds himself drawn to an idea, which he indicates rather than develops, an essentially theatrical idea: to the extent that history is theatre, then repetition, along with the tragic and the comic within repetition, forms a condition of movement under which the 'actors' or the 'heroes' produce something effectively new in history). The theatre of repetition is opposed to the theatre of representation, just as movement is opposed to the concept and to representation which refers it back to the concept. In the theatre of repetition, we experience pure forces, dynamic lines in space which act without intermediary upon the spirit, and link it directly with nature and history, with a language which speaks before words, with gestures which develop before organized bodies, with masks before faces, with spectres and phantoms before characters - the whole apparatus of repetition as a 'terrible power'.[54]

Here Deleuze posits repetition as the site of emergence of the new. Repetition occurs out of, and as difference. Deleuze is thinking pure multiplicity in this way, as opposed to Hegel's dialectic, which is concerned with the resolution of differences *in themselves,* sublating them to a higher being (the one divides into two then is sublated into one). Moreover, unlike concepts, Ideas allow us the space of difference, expressed in a multiplicity of ways. "History progresses not by negation and the negation of negation, but by affirming differences."[55]

Furthermore, Deleuze asserts the Marxist remark and takes it further by stating that those tragic and comic moments of repetition as existing for a third moment, which presents itself beyond the first two. This is the moment of production of the radically new, beyond the condition of historical action. At the beginning of *A Night at the Opera*, Otis B. Driftwood (played by Groucho Marx) was supposed to have dinner with Mrs. Claypool, but instead meets with another woman in the same restaurant that he and Mrs. Claypool agreed on. However, in a strange turn of events, they find themselves sitting back to back, Otis then joins Mrs. Claypool, and proceeds to justify his actions to her. The reason why he sat with that woman, he explains, is because she reminded him of her, and for that very reason he is now sitting here with Mrs. Claypool, because she reminds him of herself: "Your eyes, your throat, your lips! Everything about you reminds me of you. Except you."[56] To put this in Deleuzean terms, Driftwood opts for the repetition as the "*same* on the basis of the different", he chooses to sit down with a woman who repeats Mrs. Claypool, and simultaneously differs from her. Groucho's act inadvertently interprets the Deleuzean Idea: Mrs. Claypool not as the concept which has a single identity (representation), but rather that which is not representable, the being of becoming. The first confrontation of the two at the restaurant is tragic, Mrs. Claypool tells Driftwood that she has been tediously waiting for him for several hours now, to which he responds by saying: "yes, with your back to me. When I invite a woman to dinner I expect her to look at my face. That's the price she has to pay."[57] The second is comic, Driftwood, equipped with ludicrousness, attempts to escape his entanglement (that Mrs. Claypool caught him there), and consequently those two moments create the condition for the third and most important, that of the Idea as the eternal return.[58] It is at this moment that Deleuze turns to the Nietzsche:

> Eternal return cannot mean the return of the identical because it presupposes a world (that of the will to power) in which all previous identities have been abolished and dissolved. Returning is being, but only the being of becoming. The eternal return does not bring back 'the same', but returning constitutes the only Same of

> that which becomes. Returning is the becoming-identical of becoming itself. Returning is thus the only identity, but identity as a secondary power; the identity of difference, the identical which belongs to the different, or turns around the different. Such an identity, produced by difference, is determined as 'repetition'. Repetition in the eternal return, therefore, consists in conceiving the same on the basis of the different.[59]

Nietzsche's notion regards reality as an uninterrupted state of becoming, and thus it asserts the nature of pure difference. In other words, eternal recurrence upholds both difference and repetition, since it is the repetition of that which differs *from itself*—only what differs returns in this third moment. Therefore, eternal return is an affirmation of difference, as opposed to the Hegelian negation which is an activity of representation and the sublation. The first moment of the May 1968 events was characterized by a series of student protests and occupations; the workers joined forces and supported the students with nationwide strikes. The second was De Gaulle's farcical elections, which not only restored the Gaullist party, but also rendered it more powerful than ever.[60] Right after this moment, the protestors were struck with despair and fatigue, and the spirit of the revolution slowly dissipated. The revolts of Paris '68 had an egalitarian and anti-hierarchical rhetoric, it sought to find a way out of the deadlock of alienation and oppression, of social organizations and structures. One of its objectives was decentralization of economic and political power, but the very regime it opposed had won the elections and returned to repeat the old but in a new manner. This new manner is the new universal spirit of capitalism which emerged out of 1968. This new spirit of capitalism absorbed all critical ideas and objectives of the revolts, thus presenting itself as the liberating solution from the outworn tropes of left and right institutions. Dialectically, it is a sublation of both as an encompassing signifier of everything and nothing. We have come to know this spirit as the postmodern. Jean Francois Lyotard describes the "postmodern condition" as the end of the modern pursuit of progress—characterized by constantly seeking change—where constant change has become the existing state of affairs.[61] However, postmodernity to Schirmacher "means the cultural diagnosis that sees traditional orientations as devalued, without itself being able to offer a new world view."[62] What this means is that the postmodern condition accounts for the infinite number of representations to be produced, (presenting itself as the libertarian revolution, where everything goes) whilst practically they are all representations of the same identity, nothing radically new is produced. Schirmacher adds, we are "waiting in the Heideggerian sense 'without expectation' for something 'beyond postmodernity', for the true concept of a *Lebenswelt* (life-world) that strikes us every day as increasingly uncanny."[63]

May 1968 sought difference as decentering in their demand to abolish inauthentic social organizations and hierarchal structures of power, in hopes that this would lead to the emergence of multiplicities as divergence. In this very sense, the revolutionary events of Paris '68 contained the possibility of an eternal return, a repetition beyond representation, a site for the intensive differences to become extensive. After all there was truth in the protestors' slogan to be realistic, and demand the impossible.[64] The events practically failed to grasp this third moment of repetition, to realize the dream of difference; they ended up as a declaration for the end of history, or at least the end of modernity.[65] Schirmacher suggests that history has reached its end because there has never been a history, but only ever the "eternal return" of the same.[66] Schirmacher's reference to Nitetzsche is apropos, and in the same fashion I am considering the Idea of revolution beyond its historical representations.

In the introduction to the DVD release of his film *The Grin Without a Cat*, Chris Marker confesses that upon hearing his friends revel in making the revolution, he heard a representation, "a sort of sexy way to christen the true transformations of thought or mores that unfolded before us, which where not negligible, and would leave traces."[67] Today, based on his recollections of the revolts, Marker asserts that nobody had actually set a plan of action to seize power, although the partisans of '68 thought about it, talked about it, and more importantly dreamt about it. Marker concludes by saying that "revolution was in the air, and had to be, like the grin of the Cheshire cat."[68] Marker adds that one would always see that grin, but never see the cat.

The crucial point to be made is that revolution is a repetition insofar as what is eternal in the revolutionary gesture, and it is this recurrence which should be considered as the Idea. In this regard, my premise has been in order to consider revolution proper, we have to demand to see the cat. Faced with revolution, we should not attempt to deal with its possible solutions or representations, since "all attempts at a solution up until now have failed, every solution, upon closer inspection, turns out to be the entrance into a problem labyrinth with no way out."[69]

Heidegger and Creative Repetition

Martin Heidegger suggests the temporality of *Dasein* is circular, it moves from the future by way of the past and towards the present. First, let us start with the past, that in between, the "through". Heidegger does not argue for passing down past interpretations as is onto the present, rather for the past conditions and situations to be analyzed in the present for the possibilities that have been there, but are yet to be realized. Even in this "extraction" of possibilities from the past, Heidegger's aim is the possibilities of the future, the retrieval of unrealized potentiality to be realized. The sole purpose for the having been (*gewesene*) becomes inherent in the role of the past as the provider of unfulfilled possibilities:

> The resoluteness which comes back to itself and hands itself down (Die auf sich zurückkommende, sich überliefernde Entschlossenheit), then becomes the *repetition* of a possibility of existence that has come down to us (*Wiederholung* einer überkommenen Existenzmöglichkeit). *Repeating is handing down explicitly* (Die *Wiederholung ist die ausdröckliche Überlieferung*)—that is to say, going back into the possibilities of the Dasein that has-been-there. The authentic repetition of a possibility of existence that has been—the possibility that Dasein may choose its hero—is grounded existentially in anticipatory resoluteness; for it is in resoluteness that one first chooses the choice which makes one free for the struggle of loyally following in the footsteps of that which can be repeated.[70]

Heidegger thus delineates the past, not as the aim of the possibilities of *Dasein*, but always as a stepping stone for the present realization of future possibilities. "The repeating of that which is possible does not bring again something that is 'past', nor does it bind the Present back to that which has already been outstripped."[71] In other words, according to Heidegger, the proper function of *Dasein* is the realization of future possibilities in the present by way of the having been (*gewesene*), whose role is to scrutinize the past for lost possibilities.

In order to clarify Heidegger's notion of repetition, I will resort to a valid reasoning; Macquarrie and Robinson, the first translators of *Sein und Zeit* into English, posit in their notes:

> While we usually translate 'wiederholen' as 'repeat', this English word is hardly adequate to express Heidegger's meaning. Etymologically, 'wieder-holen' means 'to fetch again'; in modern German usage, however, this is expressed by the cognate separable verb 'wieder . . . holen', while 'wiederholen' means simply 'to repeat' or 'do over again'. Heidegger departs from both these meanings, as he is careful to point out. For him 'wiederholen' does not mean either a mere mechanical repetition or an attempt to reconstitute the physical past; it means rather an attempt to go back to the past and retrieve former *possibilities*, which are thus 'explicitly handed down' or 'transmitted.' [72]

For Heidegger, repetition is the handing-over of possibilities from the past to the present. In this sense, it is not the intent of Heidegger to reestablish the past as is in the present, nor should we mistake it as making the present correspond with the past. Put simply, Heidegger's repetition invites us to understand the past rather than to recollect it, therefore, repetition is primarily directed towards the future rather than backward.[73] The possibilities from the past are handed down and affirmed in a movement towards creative actualization.

In this particular sense, one should today repeat the revolution, not in order to do the same today as was done in the past, but to repeat, in the manner of extracting the non realized possibilities of the Idea of revolution, "as a struggle between the future and the past." [74]

“Real without being actual, ideal without being abstract.”

— Marcel Proust, *Le Temps Retrouvé*

4. The Virtual and The Actual of Revolution

The Virtual for Deleuze: Multiplicities and Particle Physics

So far my claim has been that repetition and radical change are intertwined, since it is only from repetition that the truly new occurs. In order to affirm this premise, I will interpret it in terms of the difference between the virtual and the actual. According to Deleuze, the virtual and the actual are two inextricable characteristics of the real. The actualization of the real is inherent in the state of affairs, representations of the Idea as such, whereas the virtual is the nonrepresentable singularities which belongs to the pure past—and by pure Deleuze designates the past that can never be fully present, in line with the Heideggerian notion of past. The virtual is capable of conveying the actual without concurring with it or ever resembling its actualization in any way.

Nevertheless, the virtual is delineated in three different manners across Deleuze's writings: as élan vital[75] in his reading of Bergson, as the Idea in his seminal *Difference and Repetition,* and finally as an *event.* All three are pertinent to my argument.

First, is Deleuze's formulation of the virtual in terms of the Bergsonian élan vital. This understanding stems from a consideration of the actualization of the present, as that past which was never present. Again, one should not reduce this to a reification of the past in the present.

The distinction should be made here between what Deleuze labels as the "pure" past versus the "virtual" past. The "pure" past is the site of has been actualizations, and attempted solutions/ representations, whereas the "virtual" is the plenum of differentiated intensities. It is this virtual that Deleuze and Bergson designate as the past that was never present, as the élan vital, the vital force which acts as the inherently differentiated dynamic of the real, thus always self-actualizing in truly new unprecedented differentiations.

Second, Deleuze identifies the virtual as characteristic of the Idea throughout *Difference and Repetition*. The Idea as such is a problem, "whereby the diverse actualizations of the virtual are understood as solutions."[76] Therefore, problems bear no resemblance to their solution or representation in the real:

> Kant never ceased to remind us that Ideas are essentially 'problematic'. Conversely, problems are Ideas..... Kant even refers to Ideas as problems 'to which there is no solution'. By that he does not mean that Ideas are necessarily false problems and thus insoluble but, on the contrary, that true problems are Ideas, and that these Ideas do not disappear with 'their' solutions, since they are the indispensable condition without which no solution would ever exist....
>
> The Idea is thus defined as a structure. A structure or an Idea is a 'complex theme', an internal multiplicity—in other words, a system of multiple, non-localizable connections between differential elements which is incarnated in real relations and actual terms.[77]

Consequently, reading revolution in terms of the Deleuzean Idea does not relegate it to a plan of action, or a political resolution, in not reducing revolution to a solution in the actual, but considering it as the problem, an internal multiplicity.

And finally, Deleuze presents the virtual as an event by way of his notion of "sense":

> Sense is both the expressible or the expressed of the proposition, and the attribute of the state of affairs. It turns one side toward things, and another side toward propositions. But it cannot be confused with the proposition which expressed it any more than with the state of affairs or the quality which the proposition denotes. It is exactly the boundary between propositions and things.[78]

Deleuze argues that sense is not external to the proposition conveying it, yet at the same time it should not be mistaken for the proposition. Additionally, sense should not be reduced to a process of semblance or identification with given states of affairs, nor should it be mistaken for or associated with any traits, or characteristic relations belonging to these states. The field of sensation persists in what comes prior to states of affairs, in what is felt and experienced before cognition interferes. Sense is at the foundation of perception, which in turn ushers the creation of events. On this subject, sense introduces the untimely nature of the virtual as "the impassive and dynamic aspects of multiplicities in the process of actualization."[79]

Alain Badiou "extracted" from *The Logic of Sense* what he calls "the four Deleuzean axioms of the event."[80] For my consideration, the second axiom is pertinent, which according to Badiou is that "the event is always that which has just happened and that which is about to happen, but never that which is happening."[81]

According to Badiou, Deleuze posits the event as the amalgamation of past and future, and in this sense, "the event is not what takes place between a past and a future, between the end of a world and the beginning of another. It is rather encroachment and connection: it realizes the indivisible continuity of virtuality."[82]

What that means it that the event brings forth a continuity from the future to the past. It is not the present, as what is, "but that which, in what happens, has become and will become."[83]

The Deleuzean event as such, rejects any reduction of the present as a passage between the past and the future, alternately; the present should not be understood as a space of separation, a gap. As such this notion is twofold: the first is the imperative that there is no present, the event conjugates the past and the future as the present, and the second where there is nothing but the present.

Badiou proceeds to invert the axioms in order to elucidate his own understanding of the event, the second axiom hence becomes: "The event would not be the inseparable encroachment of the past on the future, or the eternally past being of the future."[84]

Badiou advocates we view the event as a "vanishing mediator"[85]. The event should be considered as an intemporal point, which separates both the one that has been and the one that will be. Consequently, the event opens up the possibility of another time, as the new present. "The event is neither past nor future, rather a rupture that makes us present to the present."[86]

In July 2012, a team of researchers and physicists declared the discovery of a Higgs-like particle. The search for the Higgs particle has been arduous, since it is a highly unstable particle, and is only detectable through its daughter products. Moreover, the Higgs particle has zero electric charge, and no intrinsic spin, which enables an array of particles to uniformly occupy a space. This accumulation forms the Higgs field that might appear as pure vacuum, however it is not. Paradoxically, in spite of the fact that the Higgs particles are very unstable, being distributed in space renders them stable via their mutual interactions. Noticeable Higgs particles are only so due to them being perturbations in the uniform field.

Scientists at CERN in Switzerland have been attempting to produce Higgs particles using a hadron collider, where high-energy protons are made to move in opposite direction of each other traveling at the speed of light. As they cross path, the protons collide at varying sections, spawning "many stable or near-stable particles, such as electrons, positrons, pi mesons, photons, protons, antiprotons, and other possibilities."[87] Evidence for the presence of Higgs particles will be confirmed by the emergence of other distinct particles within the collision, due to the Higgs production and decay. Gluons within the moving protons undergo a quantum vacuum fluctuation, that is, their inherent energy temporarily changes at that given point, but only for an insignificant amount of time. This is enough to allow the formation of virtual singularities. These virtual singularities, as particle and its anti-particle, pair promptly merge back together forming a Higgs, which likewise breaks down by transforming into a pair of virtual particles, which eventually stabilize as two photons.

Of all the process described so far, scientists can only account for the two photons that emerge, and since such an occurrence is unusual, one can discern the existence of the Higgs particle by measuring its yield against the possibility of emerging particles.[88]

Briefly put, at an intemporal instant, where gluons undergo quantum fluctuations, pure difference (the virtual) emerges as a process that establishes both a particle and its anti-particle and transforms them into a Higgs particle; as a result we obtain the uniform space that is the Higgs field. In this sense, such a space is the space of multiplicity, which through repetition gives way to photons. The beauty of the above example resides in that fact that it puts into perspective, and in practical physical terms, Deleuze's three readings of the virtual. First, the emergence of virtual particles had to be repeated in order for us to obtain photons, the atemporal instant acting as the élan vital, thus rendering change possible, where at a given point in space singularities emerge. Then, the Higgs particle acts as the vanishing mediator which negotiates the relationship between the particle and its anti-particle as it disappears.

Vanishing Mediator, and the Re-actualization of the Virtual

I digress to clarify the notion of vanishing mediator. Žižek relates the production of a vanishing mediator to an imbalance between form and content, or to put it in Deleuzean, and more relevant terms, an imbalance between the Idea and its solutions. Representations or solutions bear no resemblance to the Idea; therefore the Idea is repeated, "vibrating at the threshold of a given form", until the New eventually emerges as pure difference in the virtual. [89]

Finally, the Higgs field as the event by way of Badiou presents us with the present as the site of the New; there will be no return to the gluons, instead unstable Higgs particles will emerge against the uniform background, and give way to the possibility of another time, as the *Geworfenheit* (throwness) of the Idea into the world.[90] In that respect, a throw should not be reduced to a plan of action; rather what renders that plan possible.

For the New to emerge, change should occur on the virtual level, that is to say, radical change only exists not when something reorganizes itself into something else, as an enhanced sameness in its actualization, rather when "the virtual support of the actual changes, and this change occurs precisely in the guise of a repetition in which a thing remains the same in its actuality."[91]

On this account, "pure difference is not actual, it does not concern different actual properties of a thing or among things, its status is purely virtual, it is a difference which takes place at its purest precisely when nothing changes in actuality, when, in actuality, the same thing repeats itself."[92]

The relationship between the virtual and the actual should never be understood as one of sameness, since by doing so we are relegating repetition to a self-repeating gesture of the same.

The Reality of the Virtual: Spriggs and Strata-Linear Perspective

The work of Mancunian Artist David Spriggs conflates disparate parts into an actualized whole. Spriggs utilizes a technique he calls "strata-linear perspective."[93] He begins by airbrushing shapes on separate Mylar sheets, which are eventually layered together in order to create spatial images. "The shapes on the layered Mylar all point inward towards a single vanishing point. This enables him to expand the conventional two-dimensional linear perspective by spreading it across parallel planes, thus creating actual depth. The depth is amplified by the virtual image created by his layered sheets, and the heraldingly recursive effect created by the reflection of the mylar, which expands one point linear perspective towards a vanishing mediator."[94] The final encounter with his work, as one would view exhibited art, is frontal. Consequently, what we see is nothing actual, but rather the pure virtuality actualized. Moreover, Spriggs does not attempt to conceal his techniques, for the work is exhibited in its entirety. By walking around the work, one can identify and carefully scrutinize the individual sheets and what is airbrushed on them. In this way, Spriggs is displaying the infinite potential of the virtuality of shapes, out of which the final form is actualized. This movement around the work instigates a shift, and an eventual rupture at the ontological level of being; as we move the form moves with us, what we see is the becoming form. With every time that we move, we are compelled to look again, repeating our looking. At each given moment, his work appears to us, but its form does not fully actualize. We are compelled to move again, and at every given moment we see something different. Spriggs'ss virtual environments "create an illusion of physical presence without physicality."[95] Put succinctly, the physicality of Spriggs's works exists in the realm of the *noumena*, the physicality is never fully actualized, instead by repeating our looking, we are able to develop new perceptions, or to see the work in a multiplicity of perspectives. What Spriggs's work reveals to us is the impossible phenomena, as I have discussed it in the first part of this text, the phenomena excluded from our symbolically constituted reality "an Idea, open to the unknown, a trans full of undreamt of qualities."[96] Spriggs attests to the surge of pure becoming, the virtual multiplicities, out of which determinate form can actualize.

The Deleuzean Plane of Immanence: Differential Relations and Precedence of the Idea

I now turn to Deleuze's notion of the plane of immanence, the field of originary difference that generates actuality. Moreover, the plane of immanence of Ideas, which Deleuze denotes as this field, "contain all the varieties of differential relations and all the distributions of singular points coexisting in diverse orders 'perplicated' in one another."[97] As a result Ideas, have precedence over their phenomena, since it is only through actualization that the phenomena are formed. In other words, the differentiations become concrete through the process of actualization via a 'perplication' of the continuous field of immanence, the cutting up of this continuous field at given points, which in turn produces actual being. In Deleuzean terms, actualization is "the production of finite engendered affirmations which bear upon the actual terms which occupy these places and positions, and upon the real relations which incarnate these relations and these functions".[98]

Deleuze refers to this field as the virtual/Ideal. Although the plane coincides with actuality, it should not be mistaken for or reduced to that actuality, it is not contained within it, but this actual itself is produced by the plane of immanence. It is the "groundless ground"[99] of the world and everything that moves in it. Deleuze writes, "the reality of the virtual is structure. We must avoid giving the elements and relations which form a structure an actuality which they do not have, and withdrawing from them a reality which they have."[100]

What constitutes the virtual for Deleuze is the non-localizable problematic structures of Ideas (as multiplicities). They are far from being negative propositions, or representations of actual state of affairs, instead they are "positively" or "progressively" determined as reciprocal relations of differentiated elements in mobile systems. More precisely, they consist of differentiated elements or "emissions of singularities" that "possess a mobile, immanent principle of auto-unification, radically distinct from fixed and sedimentary distributions." [101]But these problematic Ideas also possess the capacity to be actualized—they seek "solutions"—through intensive processes of differentiation.

In connection with the point previously mentioned, the reality of the virtual resides in its structure, one that is immanently determined, and formed from the differential elements, the relations of differentiations, and the singular points of emergence of these relations.

Moreover, every real object or thing has a virtual content. It is through actualization that the virtual is further differentiated and determined in accordance with actual conditions. "The virtual must be defined as strictly a part of the real object—as though the object had one part of itself in the virtual into which it is plunged as though into an objective dimension".[102]

Laconically put, as the virtual is accomplished by the process of actualization, this process conveys the actualized back into the plane of immanence. Therefore, the actualized is incorporated within this field, and can always become actualized in a different manner, as something else, that which is differentiated by repetition, through its interaction with other particles. The pair of particle and its anti-particle (virtual particles) becomes through the process of actualization a Higgs particle in the Higgs field. Unstable singularities that are differentiated across the field's background actualize as something else, whilst going back to the virtual, to become photons. And in the same sense, Spriggs's Mylar shapes actualize as the image of perception, but as soon as we move, our perception of the image changes, as it seems to actualize as something else at every given point.

The genius of Deleuze's virtual resides in its ineluctable distinction from mere possibility. The actualization of possibility is predetermined, hence it is a process of limited outcome, one of resemblance and duplication. In its actualization, the virtual has no semblance, rather it is a genuine creation in relation to the differentiations and singularities.

As Deleuze puts it, "the actualization of the virtual...always takes place by difference, divergence or differentiation. Actualization breaks with resemblance as a process no less than it does with identity as a principle. Actual terms never resemble the singularities they incarnate.... Actualization creates divergent lines which correspond to—without resembling—a virtual multiplicity".[103]

Marcel Proust explicates that borrowing elements from memory and past experience, as that which is already familiar, in an attempt to comprehend or make sense of something which is unknown, proves counterproductive, thus making this unknown even more elusive.

"Sensation however, even in its most physical form, is capable of conveying the original signature and indelibly capture the novelty of the event."[104] His hypothesis elucidates what Deleuze says in regard to the "significant differences in the virtual intensities expressed in our actual sensations. These differences do not correspond to actual recognizable differences.

That the shade of pink has changed in an identifiable way is not all-important. It is that the change is a sign of a re-arrangement of an infinity of other actual and virtual relations."[105] Moreover, Proust denies actualization any attributes of resemblance or mere mimesis, and establishes the differentiated sensations as the emergence of the truly New.

"Let me say, with the risk of appearing ridiculous, that the true revolutionary is guided by strong feelings of love. It is impossible to think of an authentic revolutionary without this quality."

— Ernesto Che Guevara, *Letters to Carlos Quijano*

5. The Enthusiasm of Revolution, or the Virtual Specter

Heidegger, Freedom, and the Throwness of Love

"The thrower of the project is thrown in his own throw. How can we account for this freedom? We cannot. It is simply a 'fact', not caused or grounded but the condition of all grounding and causation."[106]

In 2006, Apichatpong Weerasethakul wrote and directed *Syndromes and a Century*. Weerasethakul mentioned in a later interview that the film is "about transformation, and how people transform themselves for the better."[107] In addition, he states that the film's idea started with the story of his parents who were both doctors working together at a hospital. But this expanded into something bigger, as he sat down with the actors, and scouted the locations, accumulating other stories, and relations. He did not seek to limit any of those combinations, and further allowed it to flow as it pleases.

The Film starts in a rural polyclinic, which seems to be set in a picturesque environment; trees surround the place, the sun shines right through the windows into all the rooms, and there is a dominant calm that instills in the patients and staff of the medical center, the same relaxation and well-being as in us as viewers. This is cleverly devised by the director, since what is to come is a range of heart warming conversations, and romantic connotations.

At first, we are introduced to a female doctor, Toey, asking bizarre questions to an army trained doctor, Nohng, who is about to join the staff. Dr. Toey seems to have an admirer, who is sitting on the sidelines, waiting for her to be done with her interview. The interviewer seems rather flirtatious in her approach to the interviewee, yet later she seems uninterested with the affection of the fellow employee who was admiring her whilst she conducted her interview. Moreover, she puts an end to her admirer's effort once and for all, with a story about a romance she has with a local orchid expert who has visited the site of the center in search of a rare orchid.

The very same doctor, Toey, compulsively implores an old monk, who dreams of chicken and has aching joints, to cogitate about his barter of herbal infusions for prescription drugs for his temple and community. Incidentally, the monk's disciple shares an unusual attraction with the resident dentist. They speak about reincarnation, past lives, and love. The disciple shares with the dentist his intimate desire to have been a DJ instead.

The rhetoric of *Syndromes and a Century* so far seems to deal with the play of sensations, human relations, and the originary differentiation of love.The film then moves away from the warmth of the rural center, and into a neon lit city hospital.

In spite of this change, some things are repeated. An older version of the military doctor is still the subject of the same job interview, this time around however his answers are more pronounced and assertive. The same admirer is still waiting for Dr. Toey to approach her with his confession of love. We see the old monk, again still in his same predicament, trying to exchange herbal infusions for prescription medication. There exists a conceivable difference, yet both of those scenes are repetitions of the previous ones.The disciple, who in his own right has become a monk, has his eyes veiled as he lies down on the dentist's chair. Each time he attempts to remove the cloth, the dentist puts it back.

And eventually, Nohng is approached by his girlfriend who shows him photos of a building site, what she later identifies as a new hospital, in an area closer to her, as she asks him to move there next year in order for them to be together, and Nohng does not reply. An incident worth mentioning takes place when Nohng goes to visit his friends in the physiotherapy ward, where he witnesses one of the staff attempting to heal a patient using chakra healing.

In contrast to the first half of the film, the second half takes place in a cold bleak ecology. The disciple monk misses the connection with the dentist, the relationship between Nohng and his girlfriend exhibits a sense of distance, all reflective of the long artificially lit cold corridors, and the rugged concrete structures of the city around and outside the hospital. Even the hospital itself becomes the site of those trying to redeem themselves, amputees adapting to artificial limbs, trying to begin from the beginning. One has to keep in mind whilst reading this film as I am, the particularity and the conditions into which the story of the film is "thrown". The film is set in a country with a major Buddhist denomination, dealing with repetition and change in its structure and as its main themes, and as such deserves a Buddhist reading. Many of the film's scenes and conversations blatantly allude to the repetition of lives over and over again, a varied repetition, yet something seems to remain the same. The characters all are in pursuit of love, of romantic engagement. There are moments which approach overzealous joy, guided by suggestive sexuality, however none of these moments succeed in attaining such a point. This joy is virtual, since none of the characters in the film ever reach it. In the first half, they all seem to be projected towards this point; the flirtatious Dr. Troey, the polyclinic employee Toa who desires her, the old monk who is desperate for drugs, the dentist who is deeply attracted to the disciple monk, as they both feel strongly linked, and even the orchid farmer who covets the rare plant, looking for it incessantly around the premises of the clinic. They all have desires, deep drives as alive as the nature around them, and as warm as the sunlight that shines into all the rooms. Buddhism presupposes that all living beings left for themselves tend towards suffering. The primer of *Syndromes and a Century* is love, the quintessence of suffering. For someone in the pursuit of love, passionately, is surely doubtful that at any given moment he or she might get heartbroken, and suffer greatly. Nonetheless and even those who have duly suffered do not regret it one single bit, and are willing to go through the same ordeal again. There is truth in what Alain Badiou says out of personal experience about love: "There have been dramas and heart-wrenching and doubts, but I have never again abandoned a love. And I feel really assured by the fact that the women I have loved I have loved for always."[108]

In spite of the suffering and the emotional scarring, we are still compelled towards love and loving. Badiou adamantly controverts the implication made by some French dating sites that one can get love minus the suffering, ergo all of the characters in *Syndromes and a Century* are driven towards suffering. According to Buddhism, we suffer because we cannot relieve our desires, even if we acquire our objects of desire we are never satisfied. In Buddhism, the aim is to attain a state where we are free of this suffering, a state of enlightenment. The Buddhist doxa is driven by an emphasis on morality rather than ethics, in order for a Buddhist to break free with Saṃsāra, and thus end his or her suffering; they should be purified of and freed from desire.

If not, then the wheel of Dharma or Saṃsāra will govern and bind their lives, as they will continue to be born and reborn over and over again. In order to fight this compulsion to desire, and thus free ourselves from the wheel of suffering, first we must realize that our actions or Karma are immanent, what we do determines the outcome. In other words, there is no transcendence; our actions determine "progress" in attaining enlightenment. We need to curb any excessive indulging or attachment to desire, and at the same time we ought not to practice hermetic renunciation. The point here is that we should not be our desires so to speak, we are allowed to desire but not excessively. Interestingly enough, the term nirvana does not translate as enlightenment but as "blown out" or extinguished. We reach this stage of liberation from clinging to attachments, which compel us into the wheel of suffering, where ostensibly nothing much has changed, but our viewpoint. We are no longer driven by our desires, we have stepped out, and we are peacefully enlightened. Now in the second half of the film, repetition persists, we have characters who are still compelled by their desires, whilst others seem to be diverging from this path. Perhaps the most explicit message of how one should not be driven by desire, is the cloth that covers the disciple monk's eyes. He hears and converses with the dentist, but he cannot see him, and we covet what we see.[109] The monk in a properly Buddhist fashion is not abstinent or obliged by a vow of silence, however he is aided into not succumbing to desire, repeating his past predicament (in the first half of the film). What further cements this approach are the amputees who are learning to walk again. What is crucial about them is that they teach us the very core of the Buddhist axiom, that what we are attached to can be easily replaced with another, and only when we realize it that we become free. But perhaps, the most pertinent behavior in the second half is that of Nohng. There seems to be something different about him.

I believe Nohng is closer to enlightenment. He is slowly freeing himself from desire to the extent that at many instances he is distant and cold: his expressions as he rides inside the elevator, the kiss he shares with his girlfriend, and the absence of any reaction when she proposes he applies to this new hospital in her proximity. This has premise in the first half, as if he is already set on this path towards freedom—he does not succumb to the flirtations and sexual innuendos of his interviewer.

The problematic of the Idea

From a Deleuzean perspective, the attractor for all the characters in Weerasethakul's film is the Idea of love, as opposed to love in reality, its idiosyncrasies and so on, but the virtual immaterial incorporeal Idea of sensations, and pure intensities. This is, as I have already established, the anti-Hegelian argument par exellence. Hegel is unable to think pure difference, as he reduces difference to contradiction and identity. To quote Badiou again, "What kind of world does one see when one experiences it from the point of view of two and not one? What is the world like when it is experienced, developed and lived from the point of view of difference and not identity? That is what I believe love to be."[110] Hegel's contradiction is subsumed under identity, and in this sense Hegel is purely unable to think the virtual, since according to him true potential is only divulged in its actualization, However, Badiou tells us that love is a production of truth, and love in this sense is pure difference and never identity, since "actual things have an identity, but virtual ones do not, they are pure variations. An actual thing must change—become something different—in order to express something. Whereas, the expressed virtual thing does not change—only its relation to other virtual things, other intensities and Ideas changes."[111]

This is the love we encounter throughout *Syndromes and a Century*, one that is purely virtual, not the actual love that must change in order to express or represent something; friendship, care, romance, worry, interpersonal relations, mutual engagements, trust, etc. And for this reason Nohng stands out because he is not in pursuit of his own self-interest (excessive attachment, desires, libidinal pleasure). Love cures the need for such pursuits. "Provided it isn't conceived only as an exchange of mutual favors, or isn't calculated way in advance as a profitable investment... It takes us into key areas of the experience of what is difference and, essentially, leads to the idea that you can experience the world from the perspective of difference. In this respect it has universal implications."[112]

Deleuzean Ideas and the Lacanian Real

"Where there is nothing, read that I love you."

— Simone Weil

Lacan asserts that demands surpass the mere need for things, it all comes down to love. At the heart of every demand, so to speak, lies a desire, someone who is in love with another person incessantly asks the other to announce his or her love. They insist upon repetitions of the affirmation, as if no affirmation is ever quite enough. This restless desiring, as Lacan instructs us, is unquenchable—there is no telos of satisfaction. I am perpetually dissatisfied, since the love I demand in excess to the gratification of my needs, is non-objectifiable. This resonates with the Deleuzean Idea, which never resembles its solutions, and is therefore repeated. In the problematic of the Idea "the diverse actualizations of the virtual are understood as solutions,"[113] and to think of the Real as a problem means that there should be some actualization of a virtual as a kind of solution to that problem. Lacan recourses to what he calls *object a,* the virtual content of Ideas. As Deleuze tells us, the virtual is accomplished by the process of actualization, and actualizing something is differentiating it. The same goes for the Lacanian *objet a,* that which appears as a regular object is actualized as the object of desire. The Idea as Real is brought forth as a genuine creative process, where the actualization of the object of desire does not resemble the actual object, since such an actualization is not subsumed under identity.

Objet a therefore, should be thought in terms of the Deleuzean *noumena* as "the phenomena excluded from our symbolically constituted reality."[114] On the level of the actual, change does not take place, what actually occurs is a differentiated repetition of the same.

This reading is congruent with pure difference as defined and explained previously in this dissertation; a difference that "differentiates" the same object from itself, as opposed to a difference between two objects.

Lacan expounds *objet a* as the leftover, the remnant left behind by the introduction of the Symbolic in the Real, or as Žižek puts it "that unfathomable X which forever eludes the symbolic grasp and thus causes the multiplicity of symbolic perspectives." [115] As a result, this space (hole) is the very point where pure difference emerges. Žižek dubs this gap minimal difference, "a pure difference which cannot be grounded in positive substantial properties." [116] There is evidence of this minimal difference in Badiou's philosophy, especially in his formulation of the universal.

Badiou, Universality, and Minimal Difference

Badiou expounds Christianity to have raised love to the level of transcendence, as universality. Although he concurs with this immanent universality in love, he claims love to be "simply the opportunity we are given to enjoy a positive, creative, affirmative experience of difference. The Other, no doubt, but without the "Almighty-Other", without the "Great Other" of transcendence."[117]

To put it in practical terms, Badiou considers the case of sexual difference:

> The predicative particularities identifying the positions "man" and "woman" within a given society can be conceived in an abstract fashion. A general principle can be posited whereby the rights, status, characteristics and hierarchies associated with these positions should be subject to egalitarian regulation by the law. This is all well and good, but it does not provide a ground for any sort of universality as far as the predicative distribution of gender roles is concerned. For this to be the case, there has to be the suddenly emerging singularity of an encounter or declaration; one that crystallizes a subject whose manifestation is precisely its subtractive experience of sexual difference. Such a subject comes about through an amorous encounter in which there occurs a disjunctive synthesis of sexuated positions. Thus the amorous

> scene is the only genuine scene in which a universal singularity pertaining to the Two of the sexes—and ultimately pertaining to difference as such—is proclaimed. This is where an undivided subjective experience of absolute difference takes place. We all know that, where the interplay between the sexes is concerned, people are invariably fascinated by love stories; and this fascination is directly proportional to the various specific obstacles through which social formations try to thwart love. In this instance, it is perfectly clear that the attraction exerted by the universal lies precisely in the fact that it subtracts itself (or tries to subtract itself) as an asocial singularity.[118]

First of all, Badiou identifies as "particular" that which may be observed with respect to an already established description, in this case what constitutes and is identified as "man" or "woman", as cultural traits. Such predicates identify gender roles differently, and even though the law gives both genders equal rights and status, this should not be mistaken for a "universal sublation of particularity." [119]

It is only through authentic love that such universality presents itself, and it does so "not as a regularization of the particular, but as a singularity that is subtracted from identitatian predicates." [120] In other words, love as minimal difference, differentiates "man" and "woman" from their sexually predicated identity. Although love can be identifiable, nevertheless it is subtracted as the Lacanian X which forever evades symbolization, or in Badiouan terms, predicated description. As a conclusion, it is only through such singularity that the universal emerges. Thus, universal singularity does not belong to the order of being, but to that of the radically New. After all, "what does it matter how many lovers you have if none of them gives you the universe?"[121]

This is best exemplified in Jonathan Lethem's *As She Climbed Across the Table*. In a fictional university somewhere in California, Professor Soft, the head of the physics department, in an attempt to recreate the big bang, succeeds in opening up a Farhi-Guth Universe.[122] The protagonist of the novel, Phillip Engstrand, who is in love with one of the physicists at the department, refers to the experiments conducted as "the pursuit of tiny nothingness"[123], and that Soft "had the audacity to pursue a big nothingness. If his work succeeded the inflationary bubble would detach and grow into a universe tangential to ours. Another world. It would be impossible to detect, but equally real."[124] What follows is that the false vacuum would not detach, but persists, and as a result Alice, Philip's love interest, moves out of their apartment in order to stay close to the breach. Eventually nothing happens, the breach stopped being an event, not even a failure, as it stabilized into what the physicists are calling Lack. Dr. Soft explains to Philip that referring to it as a breach was a misdefinition, "it was initially accompanied by a gravity event, which in turn resulted in a time event."[125] But in its current stabilized state, it is not accompanied by any event. The presence of Lack is accountable for by particles that should be there but are not. Dr. Soft gives credence to fact that the creation event is being infinitely reproduced, repeating as it were the original experiment of creating a universe in a lab.

Alice's approaches Lack as a void intelligence. Lack selectively consumes certain objects and particles, whilst refusing others. The selections are not random, "Lack's tastes make up his being. His preference for certain particles is all there is to him. If he stops choosing he stops existing."[126] At first, Alice tried to pass a paper clip through the space where Lack is, but the paper clip dropped to the floor on the other side. She tried again, and it failed again. Then she tried with a dime and it failed to be "eaten" by Lack as well. However, Lack seems to have taken Alice and Philip's apartment key. Lack proceeds to consume anthracite, light bulbs, yellow construction paper, a photo of the president, a fertilized duck eggs, and eventually B-84, a cat. The consumption of the cat stirs up a riot on the university campus, which resembles in form and in structure, as well as in rhetoric, modern day mobilizations.

From this point onwards, the relationship between Alice and Philip starts deteriorating, she moves into the lab where Lack is and out of Philip's life. Later that day, Alice attempts entering Lack but is rejected. Alice professes her love for another to Philip, and upon Philip's inquiry about the identity of her lover she asserts it is Lack. Philip and Alice are both feeling the same thing, living on the brink of the void of unrequited love. Philip loves Alice, who does not seem to love him, but is in love with Lack. "If Alice had really climbed up on Lack's table, then he'd turned her down, hadn't he? Making things disappear was the only 'I love you' in his binary vocabulary."[127] Alice's state deteriorates after being rejected by Lack, she tries desperately to make Lack accept her, she "feeds" him paintings she did, but he consumes all except her self-portraits.

Eventually, Philip is approached by the head of an Italian research team, who were brought in to collaborate on studying Lack. The Italian physicist has a theory which he shares with Philip. He believes Lack to be a new universe that does not have intelligent life, and due to the anthropic principle[128], where the existence of a universe is strictly bound to that of conscious life, since only by being perceived by such a consciousness that the universe *is*. Since Lack does not contain any conscious life, it clings to our reality that does. Lack had acquired the personality of the first conscious being it had encountered: Alice. She has made an impression on Lack, he borrows her opinions and tastes, whereas in principle Lack should be impartially hungry, what it consumes are Alice's preferences. According to this theory, Alice is then in love with a reflection of herself, she is in a narcissistic relationship. Philip deduces that in order to test whether Alice loves him or not, he has to try and enter Lack. Being drunk right after a Christmas party at the university, he slides across the table into Lack. As soon as he is up the next day, he realizes he is in a new unstable universe, almost surreal; orange skies and skewed buildings are recreated from Alice's/Lack's preferences. He proceeds towards the Lack chamber and climbs a second time into it, only to find himself in a complete dark world. In his blind state, he is aided by two blind men, close friends of Alice, which have entered Lack believing they would be able to see in a different universe. They usher him into Lack's chamber in the lab, and for the third and final time, believing this would reinstate him into his initial reality, Philip enters Lack. Nevertheless he merges with Lack. Alice, comes over to the lab, she attempts to enter Lack one last time, she takes off all her clothes and climbs across the table to the space where Lack is: "I saw her eyes then, as she came across, and they were clear, and full of love."[129]

The corollary of Buddhism is to determine the cause of suffering, then to change the manner through which one relates to this cause. Nothing changes but the perspective of the observer. Both Philip and Alice undergo such a shift. They both suffer unjustly, victimizing themselves, each in their own manner. Philip narcissistically asks Alice how she can leave him, and why he is such a doormat. Alice on the other hand is haunted by Lack's rejection of her. But as Philip realizes around the very end, Alice is narcissus, which means that she is the object causing her own suffering. The same goes for Philip, Lack is a reflection of his self as well, his aggression towards lack is an aggression turned towards himself. Philip is "freed", he now sees things the way they really are, the truth. Once both characters realize that Lack designates that which is between identitarian predicates and the plenum from which they are enunciated, a subtracted singularity, they find true love, "as the production of truth"[130], literally becoming universal. In this precise manner, Badiou writes:

> The localization of a universal singularity, is bound up with the infinite. On this particular issue, it is possible to show that there is an essential complicity between the philosophies of finitude, on the one hand, and relativism, or the negation of the universal and the discrediting of the notion of truth, on the other. Let me put it in terms of a single maxim: The latent violence, the presumptuous arrogance inherent in the currently prevalent conception of human rights derives from the fact that these are actually the rights of finitude and ultimately—as the insistent theme of democratic euthanasia indicates—the rights of death. By way of contrast, the evental conception of universal singularities, as Jean-Francois Lyotard remarked in *The Differend*, requires that human rights be thought of as the rights of the infinite.[131]

Badiou asserts there is no truth in what is referred to as universal human rights; this universality is always reduced to the finite, since it is identified in terms of the dominant ideology. What is achieved, as a result, is a mere repetition of the existing power situation—no true emancipation, or the emergence of universality proper. "In social life, for example, what the multitude of (ideological) symbolizations-narrativizations fail to render is not society's *self-identity* but the *antagonism*, the constitutive splitting of the body politic."[132] It is not a question of struggling for the acceptance and "rights" of a certain group, but in order for the struggle to be universal, it has to be antagonistic, fighting all that within a situation prevents this equality or emancipation to emerge. In more simple terms, struggle should not be reduced to the conflict between two opposing parties, where one is to be destroyed, but to eliminate any tension or obstacle that threatens the infinite nature of its universalism.

A crucial point to be made here is how Alice and Philip address the riots following Lack's "consumption" of the cat B-84. Alice's position is self-explanatory, and on par with Badiou. She warns the protestors of their misunderstanding of the situation; they are creating a false dichotomy, something versus nothing, life versus entropy, cat versus Lack. However, with the current developments, namely Lack and what it stands for, there is a chance to go beyond such old distinctions or choosing sides of a conflict, or dichotomizing struggle. "Lack is where life and entropy can reconcile their differences."[133]

Philip posits nothing new in Lack's consumption of the cat, since "the universe is always swallowing cats, it's forever swallowing cats. To protest it like this… well, it's an act of enormous irrelevance. But it's a poor choice. There's a real confusion of symbolism here. Science, death, dollars. Lack isn't any of those things."[134] At this moment in the novel, Philip is still ignorant of the truth about Lack, the fact that Lack is a projection of both Alice and himself, and that Lack, and here comes the punchline, is not the external limitation which impedes their love, but the minimal difference. Since the beginning of the novel, Philip is looking for signs of Alice's feelings towards him. He seems to be missing her love, or in Lacanian, the symbolic order which accounts for those signs and signifiers allows Philip to say it is missing. The breach, conveniently in the novel is named Lack, a lack in the Symbolic that is, resisted symbolization, precisely since it is a traumatic eruption of the Real in the Symbolic order. With regard to the Real however, it cannot be missing. There is no lack in the Real, no lack in Lack, and this is perfectly expressed in the final act of the novel, Philip finds what he has been missing in the Symbolic, Alice's authentic love.

Hyperreality and the Passion for the Real

Alain Badiou defines *the passion for the Real* as the main attribute of the twentieth century. His formulation has premise in the aims of the century to provide the "thing itself", the realization of the New. Throughout the century, the Real was directly experienced in opposition to everyday reality. However, the century's experience of the Real was violent and destructive, since it was directed at unmasking copies, and discrediting fakes, in the search to identify the real thing.

Nevertheless, Badiou has indicated that taking the destructive path towards the Real culminates in the opposite, the passion for semblance. "The key to this reversal resides in the ultimate impossibility to draw a clear distinction between deceptive reality and some firm positive kernel of the Real: every positive bit of reality is *a priori* suspicious, since (as we know from Lacan) the Real Thing is ultimately another name for the Void."[135]

Moreover, Žižek accounts for this semblance, in a popular production approach available today on the market; products that taste, smell, feel, and are like the real thing without being the real thing: "cream without fat, beer without alcohol…" Žižek makes the analogy between such products and Virtual Reality. He posits VR as a generalization offering a product bereft of its substance. Virtual Reality in this manner, furnishes "*reality itself* deprived of the resisting hard kernel of the Real. However, at the end of this process of virtualization, the inevitable Benthamian conclusion awaits us: reality is its own best semblance,"[136] or as Badiou puts it:

"It is reality that acts as an obstacle to the discovery of the real as pure surface. Here lies the struggle against semblance." [137]

In 2012, Channel 4[138] aired a special program, that was inspired by all the global speculations, about the end of the world. The program was created and developed by the British illusionist and mentalist, Derren Brown. Brown and his team placed audition ads for an unannounced television program some months before. Having fit the criteria and the characteristics of what Brown and his team were looking for, Steven Brosnan was selected as their protagonist. Steven follows an idyllic carefree life. Brown and his team, in accordance with his family and friends, plant cameras and start secretly filming him for four weeks. Next, Brown has hackers access Steven's computer and phone in order to control and feed him news and information. Their starting premise is the prolific Perseid meteorite shower[139], which accompanies the annual passage of the Swift-Tuttle comet over Great Britain. Brown plants false news of an immanent threat, since this time around the meteorite shower seems to veil something far more dangerous behind it. Slowly, Steven starts believing that the threat is real, since his regular morning radio show is consistently discussing the shower with experts. Brown even tweets as some well known physicist that Steven is following, confirming the disaster in theory. In short, Darren Brown made it all so real for Steven to be convinced that it is. Steven is eventually lured out of his house under the false pretense that he is going to an exclusive concert by his favorite band in a secret location. Whilst on route, the apocalypse begins. The bus and its passengers dodge burning cars and theatrical explosions, a scene worthy of Hollywood's action films. Brown, who has been sitting on the bus, stands up and hypnotizes Steven. As Steven gains consciousness, he is in a hospital bed. He soon gets up and walks out of his room towards a television set in the waiting room. On the set, there is a looping public announcement broadcast by the British Army explaining what happened and warning from another more serious threat, a viral infection. Some of the rocks that hit earth have been carrying a pathogen, which turns humans into undead cannibals. In this post-apocalyptic world, Steven is shocked and he soon finds two other survivors, a little girl who lost her mother, and a Scot. They all take shelter in a former nuclear weapons site. Completely unaware of the staged spectacle, Steven is compelled to make the right decisions and to interact with the other survivors, who are actors in the show. All his attempts are directed towards joining his family, whom he knows to be alive and well in Wales—apparently all survivors were brought to the Nuclear weapons site before leaving to Wales or Scotland, the two safe zones, and they all left a message board on the fence for their loved ones who were missing. Steven has to make some serious decisions, and eventually face the zombie army in order to distract them as other survivors make it to the extraction point. He ends up sacrificing his rescue and evacuation by the army, whom he had contacted a day before using a shortwave radio, in order to save the little girl.

Darren Brown and his production team managed to create a hyperreality, staged to convince Steven that the post-apocalyptic world he lives in is the real world. Their aim was to instill change in Steven, for him to realize the value of the people around him, mainly his family, and to give him a second chance at life. However, there is a deeper meaning to the Darren Brown Special (conveniently named *Apocalypse*). In constructing this hyperreality, what Brown and his team accomplished is the uncovering of Steven's reality world as being a semblance, its best semblance. It is only through the staged end of the world that he was able to appreciate his mother, and change from leeching on his parents to taking charge of his own life. What the show has done is simply obliterate the obstacle of Steven's reality by throwing him, in the Heideggerian sense of course, back into the virtual of pure intensities. The staged *Apocalypse* evokes the notion of minimal difference. At first, when Steven wakes up to find an apocalypse has taken place, the failure of his life to persist echoes the bigger failure, which is the reason he is in this predicament. In this catastrophic space he has to change, he is forced to. Darren Brown has provided him with another chance, a repetition. It is through this repetition that the purely virtual aspect emerges, that of an ameliorated version of Steven. In this sense, Steven Brosnan does not repeat the life he had on which Derren Brown founds the pretense of his hyppereality, but Steven's reality and the hyperreal together repeat the virtual life, whose becoming is made evident in the movement from the actual reality to the staged hyperreal. *Apocalypse* retroactively interpolates into Steven's reality the possibility of a different actualization of the Idea.

Crucial to note here is that repetition:

> ...is a virtuality that is differentiated every time it is actualized. The variations, in other words, do not come from without, but express differential mechanisms which belong to the essence and origin of what is repeated. There is not an orginary "thing" (model) which could eventually be uncovered behind the disguises, displacements, and illusions of repetition (copies); rather, disguise and displacement are the essence of repetition itself, which is in itself an original and positive principle.[140]

Problems, Representations, Signs, and Love

As I stated in the introduction, my aim resides in considering revolution as the problem, as opposed to considering it as the solution to a problem. Deleuze sees solutions as endeavors to consider the 'impossible-real' of the Idea. Problems as such are universal, as I have come to demonstrate earlier with the Idea of love.

Concurrently, actual reality should be strictly comprehended as a cyclic answer, repetition, to a virtual problem. Furthermore, Deleuze posits solutions to be grasped as signs, "as problematic structure is part of objects themselves."[141] And alternately, if we were to grasp actual reality as an answer to a virtual problem, then actual reality presents itself to us as a 'sign'. There is truth in what Wolfgang Schirmacher announced during a lecture at the European Graduate School in Saas-Fee: "I have no solution, but I can make it clear how problematic it is."[142] It is in this very sense that answers are signs to the problem.

Signs for Deleuze are opposed to representations. "It is signs that expose new relations in our world, and it is the search of signs that creates the most basic meanings through which we know the world" [143] Representations are appearances or figures of objects divested of the virtual ground. Whereas signs link the object back to its virtual, placing it in closer relation to the problem/Idea.

Deleuze identifies in Proust's *In Search of Lost Time*, what he calls "signs of love". These signs "are not empty signs, standing for thought and action. They are deceptive signs which can be addressed to us only by concealing what they express: the origin of unknown worlds, of unknown actions and thoughts which give them a meaning."[144]

What Deleuze is suggesting here is precisely that these signs of love evoke an unknown, and therefore should not be reduced to representations. Representations mediate objective entities present at hand, deprived of any virtual ground or depth. Although signs are made up of actual material entities, and consequently engage in the objective entities of actions, or thought, they point out, or project, other entities and other intensities. Proust's narrator reads Albertine's glimpses and gentle touches as signs of love, only to realize that was not the case. He misinterprets her actions at the level of actuality as love. But once he realizes his misreading, he is then confronted with the problem, the fact that he wants to be more than just a friend to Albertine. Albertine's actions are signs of the problem, and only when the narrator grasps the virtual force which accompanied Albertine's actions, that he grasps the problem:

> The Christian name for this virtual force is 'love': when Christ says to his worried followers after his death "when there will be love between two of you, I will be there," he thereby asserts this virtual status.[145]

The deduction to be drawn here resides in Deleuze and Guattari's claim apropos revolution. In *What is Philosophy?* they approach revolution as a concept or event, in opposition to positing it in terms of the actual (its existence as such) within a specific place. What is vital for them is to distinguish between the actual taking place of the revolution and the event, the virtual field, which lies at the heart of revolution, and can be extracted from it. Succinctly put, revolution does not derive its sign from history with a fixed time and place, but rather, when thought as the Idea, it is that which gives to history a *becoming*. This is congruent with Badiou's notion of "subtractive path", or minimal difference; a purification of reality, through its subtraction from its apparent unity, discerning within this reality "the vanishing mediator that accounts for it. Or more specifically, what *barely* takes place differs from the place wherein it takes place. It is in the 'barely' that all the affect rests, in this immanent exception."[146]

In going back to Lethem's *As She Climbed Across the Table*, Lack as the irregularity has breached reality in the novel. It barely takes place and is expected to close. In order for the protagonist to reach the Real, he had to subtract his love from himself, from any semblance or appearance of it in reality. Lack opens up a place to begin anew. Similarly, *Apocalypse* enabled Steven to subtract the better version of himself, thus driving him towards radical change.

Philip lacked, so to speak, when his body was not there anymore, and he emerged as the void, as the event. He did not deny what happened as the truth, nor did he try to force things back to what they were, on the contrary he embraced the truth as such and began "drawing the consequences."[147] Philip was faithful to the event, as he started structuring the situation from the new viewpoint:

> It is to posit revolution as plane of immanence, infinite movement and absolute survey, but to the extent that these features connect up with what is real here and now in the struggle against capitalism, relaunching new struggles whenever the earlier one is betrayed. As Kant showed, the concept of revolution exists not in the way in which revolution is undertaken in a necessarily relative social field but in the "enthusiasm" with which it is thought on an absolute plane of immanence, like a presentation of the infinite in the here and now, which includes nothing rational or even reasonable. The concept frees immanence from all the limits still imposed on it by capital (or that it imposed on itself in the form of capital appearing as something transcendent).[148]

A crucial point to be made here is Deleuze's use of 'concept'. Having dismissed concepts altogether in his previous work, especially in Difference and Repetition, which lays the ground to his ontology, it appears that by way of Guattari he reinstates it.

First of all, concept should not be read as the Deleuzean Idea, "as if Deleuze had indeed been giving a theory of concepts all along, but used the term Idea to emphasize his break with previous accounts of the conceptual."[149] Falling into this misinterpretation equates Deleuze to Proust's narrator and his misinterpretation of Albertine's actions as love. In Deleuze's case, it is misreading 'concept' in terms of the virtual continuum that underlies the production of the actual. This endows beings, who are able to think conceptually, with an ontological privilege of accessing the impossible-real.

On the contrary, 'concept' should be read in this context as a re-actualization of the virtual field of immanence that is revolution. It is in support of this reading that Deleuze alludes to Kant. What Deleuze and Guattari mean is that the re-actualization of revolution is not to be equated with the actual order of things, or what is happening in actuality only, but that for revolution to be re-actualized there has to be a virtual field. This field of differences only persists as a specter co-occuring with actualities and their interpenetration.

In other words, the Idea of the revolution (and its virtual continuum) emerges only by way of its actualization. However, the true "success of a revolution resides only in itself, precisely in the vibrations, clinches, and openings it gave to men and women at the moment of its making and that composes in itself a monument that is always in the process of becoming."[150] It is this opening up that is brought forth by the actualization of the revolution which should be grasped as the immanent exception, or to call it by its true name; radical change and the emergence of the New.

"La beauté et l'infini veulent être regardés sans voiles."

— Victor Hugo, *Post Scriptum de ma Vie*

"Are these the shadows of the things that will be or are they the shadows of the things that may be, only?"

— Charles Dickens, *Christmas Carol*

"All revolutions are the sheerest fantasy until they happen; then they become historical inevitabilities."

— David Mitchell, *Cloud Atlas*

6. Revolution and Time

Based on my arguments so far, I posit the revolutionary event as a specter, namely the virtual specter of the Idea. By that very fact, the actualization of the Idea of revolution, can be considered as an in-between, meaning it ascribes to the state of affairs without being caused by them. The temporality of such an actualization is consequently for Deleuze and for my consideration, an opening in the present, as the infinite that takes place here and now, an a-temporal present as the possibility of another time.

I will discuss in this section, the temporality of the actualization of revolution (its relation to history, and its validity in becoming revolutionary), while the next section will be dealing with the "in-between" notion of the revolution in terms of spacing.

Repetition, Heidegger's Resoluteness, and the Continuity of the Virtual

So far, I have established the notion of repetition as a repetition with difference. Moreover, this pure difference is prominent in the movement of the actualized through the virtual field, to be re-actualized in a radically new state. This movement is that of pure becoming, the virtual multiplicities, out of which determinate form can actualize. Actualization is a "sign" (Deleuzean) of the Idea, since each actualization of the Idea is a solution to its problematic. Nonetheless this process of actualization is never predetermined in the virtual. The virtual as creative emergence manifests each actualization as radically new, without resemblance or precedence. This movement of repetition and difference is not yet a being, but rather it is the reprisal of being, the continuous becoming of the

Idea. In other words, the virtual is an opening for the present to reprise a differentiated being, a being that was betrayed by its past actualization, and at the same time to realize future possibilities. Let me recapitulate; through the repetition of the actual, the virtual enables the emergence of the radically new via a process of differentiation, which synthesizes the past and the future, or as Badiou suggests, as the "encroachment and connection."[151]

This continuity of the virtual is not the intrinsic present, but the resoluteness of what becomes and will become.

I recourse to Heidegger's notion of resoluteness, as an opening up. It is in *Being and Time* that Heidegger writes about the present, or what he refers to as the *authenti*c present, the present held in authentic temporality, as a resolute rupture. Resoluteness is quite similar to the continuity of the virtual in Deleuze. This resoluteness is not simply the actual present, but that which repeats the past as it is projected towards the future. This should not be misread as whilst considering the immanent in the future, namely that which is in the future a continuity of the present—the inevitable death, one recollects what was earlier present in the past, that which is no longer present, in the generic sense of life flashing before our eyes as we are confronted with death. In succumbing to this reduction, there is a sense of disinterest in the actual present—the two rebuttals against this reduction are Deleuze's own refusal to consider repetition as cyclical return of habit, or as recollection of memory. Approaching time as circular, and as a result repetition as the cyclical return of sameness, has been so far disproven. This repetition produces mere habit. The second consideration is that of the Kantian linearity of time. This approach is devoid of the cyclic, and thus nothing returns. Memory is thus applied to make sense of the present by means of the past. In other words, this process identifies the present by means of the past. Hence, there is no differentiation. The present is simply experienced through the past.

On the other hand, this resoluteness should be conceived as an opening, a "time spacing".

Heidegger coins the term "time-space" in order to designate time that opens up, the intrinsic characteristic of time as *Einräumen*[152], or creating space. It is that which creates a space, the present, not through emptying it, but in filling it up with the actualization of the *having-been*, and the anticipation of the future. This present is an eternally present.

History and Becoming

The emergence of the new for Deleuze always prevails over the historical context:

> The thing is, I became more and more aware of the possibility of distinguishing between becoming and history. It was Nietzsche who said that nothing important is ever free from a "nonhistorical cloud." This isn't to oppose eternal and historical, or contemplation and action: Nietzsche is talking about the way things happen, about events themselves or becoming. What history grasps in an event is the way it's actualized in particular circumstances; the event's becoming is beyond the scope of history. History isn't experimental, it's just the set of more or less negative preconditions that make it possible to experiment with something beyond history. Without history the experimentation would remain indeterminate, lacking any initial conditions, but experimentation isn't historical. In a major philosophical work, Clio, Peguy explained that there are two ways of considering events, one being to follow the course of the event, gathering how it comes about historically, how it's prepared and then decomposes in history, while the other way is to go back into the event, to take one's place in it as in a becoming, to grow both young and old in it at once, going through all its components or singularities. Becoming isn't part of history; history amounts only the set of preconditions, however recent, that one leaves behind in order to 'become,' that is, to create something new. This is precisely what Nietzsche calls the Untimely...It's fashionable these days to condemn the horrors of revolution. It's nothing new; English Romanticism is permeated by reflections on Cromwell very similar to present-day reflections on Stalin. They say revolutions turn out badly. But they're constantly confusing two different things, the way revolutions turn out historically and people's revolutionary becoming. These relate to two different sets of people. Men's only hope lies in a revolutionary becoming: the only way of casting off their shame or responding to what is intolerable.[153]

Deleuze is clear in his approach to history. Even though what takes place does so against the backdrop of a historical context, or in a given particular circumstance, what history grasps is the actualization and not the virtual field, or the Idea for that matter. The virtual that becomes eludes the historical grip. Around the end of the excerpt, Deleuze turns towards revolution.

He makes a separation between the actual revolution, what happens on the streets, the violence, its idiosyncrasies, the slogans, mobilizations, and so on, and what he calls "revolutionary becoming". This becoming is precisely the virtual specter of the Idea, which is beyond history, as the Nietzschean untimely. Its "untimeliness" resides first in the virtual field acting on history, as another time not of the historical context, and second as the opening unto the atemporal infinite virtuality of the Idea. What becomes does so always by way of repetition; for something new to emerge, it has to emerge through repetition. Moreover, what emerges as new is new eternally.

Becoming-Active: Malabou on Deleuze, and Eternal Return

In his book on Nietzsche, Deleuze claims repetition as "being of difference as such, or the eternal return."[154] Deleuze adds that eternal return is not the return of the same, it should never be understood as cyclical, the axiom of habit. It is not the identical which returns, but that which is different. The vital point here is to view eternal return as the realization of Deleuze's virtual. "The subject of the eternal return is not the same but the different, not the similar but the dissimilar, not the one but the many."[155] If only that which is different returns, then this process is an affirmation of difference, a creative selection:

> The eternal return produces becoming-active. It is sufficient to relate the will to nothingness to the eternal return in order to realize that reactive forces do not return. However far they go, however deep the becoming-reactive of forces, reactive forces will not return. The small, petty, reactive man will not return. Affirmation alone returns, this that can be affirmed alone returns, joy alone returns. Everything that can be denied, everything that is negation, is expelled due to the very movement of the eternal return. We were

> entitled to dread that the combinations of nihilism and reactivity would eternally return too. The eternal return must be compared to a wheel; yet, the movement of the wheel is endowed with centrifugal powers that drive away the entire negative. Because Being imposes itself on becoming, it expels from itself everything that contradicts affirmation, all forms of nihilism and reactivity: bad conscience, ressentiment, we shall witness them only once...The eternal return is the Repetition, but the Repetition that selects, the Repetition that saves. Here is the marvelous secret of a selective and liberating repetition.[156]

Catherine Malabou explicates the moment in Deleuze as "the differentiant [différenciant] of the difference that operates an energetic but not a logical division between that which returns and that which fails to return. A principle of selection that separates the affirmation from what it is not."[157]

It is rather obvious that Deleuze's notion of eternal return is deployed against the Hegelian contradiction and negation. For Deleuze, what eternal return provides is the liberation from predetermined identity, and cyclic repetition of the same. It is referred to as becoming-active, not reactive, not oppositional or contradictory, nor negating, and hence non-identitarian. This emergence is not governed by a specific moment, the multiplicity emerges neither as "self-contradictory nor self-overcoming".[158] And it is repetition that safeguards such an emergence from the trope of reducing it to sameness, since "eternal return is a thought of synthesis...the principle of the reproduction of diversity as such, of the repetition of difference."[159]

As Malabou asserts, this eternal return is what constantly renders and assures the operation of differentiation. What serves as selection for eternal return is the will to power: "whatever you will, will it in such a way that you also will its eternal return."[160] It is for this very reason that willing selects through differentiation all that is active, and non-identical, as creation.

Therefore, the atemporal opening unto the virtual field, where differentiation occurs through repetition, is not a moment that reflects its historical context, nor the time and space where it emerges, but precisely the creative moment, the affirmation and production of something new.

Creative Evolution towards the Nomadic Time

Active-becoming is essentially a creative process, one that is free from the predetermined and the representational, albeit its actualization takes place in a given context. It is creation in that which is not yet that achieves novelty through the virtual.

The virtual, thus is the field of creativity of new possibilities. This describes a being that reprises itself over and over again, an eternally coming into being; a becoming, and herein resides the creative power of the virtual. The experience of the actual as the real time, this moment, is lacking, this actuality is limited in its future possibilities, what is already given is what will be. Instead, it is only by way of the virtual, what has not yet unfolded, that this creative process produces infinite multiplicities and possibilities. Deleuze's main issue with the actual and its temporality, is its reduction of the idea and its eternal to resemblence. The same thing that is now will be in the future, or what is actual in this moment will be realized in the future. This renders the future a simplistic continuity of the present, and by doing so reduces repetition to the cycle of habit, where nothing new can ever emerge, all is the same all is predetermined. The virtual for Deleuze creates its own actual. Michael Hardt presents this "actualization of being as a dynamic and original emanation, as a *creative evolution* free from the ordering restraints of both Platonic finalism (final cause) and the realization of the possible (formal cause)."[161]

Moreover, this becoming is not transcendence; it is neither beyond nor outside, but perfectly inscribed in the plane of immanence as previously discussed. What Deleuze urges us to do is to free the future from what is given in the actual present.

The obvious question is how to free revolution from what is already predetermined, from it being the realization of given grounded structures, since its very formalization, in this respect, delineates a conformism to a previous model. The answer is of course Deleuzean, it is the revolutionary becoming that should be considered, that active becoming which creatively differentiates. In order to do so, I assign to the time of revolution Deleuze's concept of "nomadism". Nomadic time is creative time; this means that the revolutionary event continuously varies the in-between points that constitute the path of the future. Instead of having a converging future, what is present will be realized in this futuristic point, this creative nomadic movement, whilst acknowledging the future, infinitesimally differentiates any given actual point, thus rendering the future completely unknown, a yet to come.

"The future you have tomorrow, won't be the same future you had yesterday."

— Chuck Palahniuk, *Rant*

DeLanda, Deleuze, the Catastrophic, and the Future to Come

Manuel DeLanda, in his reading of the Deleuzean becoming, warns against the impossibility of true innovation, if the future were to be considered as " all that is already given in the past, and merely that modality of time where previously determined possibilities become realized."[162] DeLanda finds in Deleuze a solution that safeguards against such a mistaking of the future; positing a truly open ended model of the future, where "the past and present are not only pregnant with possibilities which become real, but with virtualities which become actual."[163]

If the future is a mere realization of what is predetermined, or a continuity of what is given, such a future can never be open, and as such there can never be something new, since it is reduced to mere reification. The process of actualization of the virtual is what ensures the emergence of the new, and thus an open becoming:

> It is perhaps necessary to free the value of the future from the value of 'horizon' that traditionally has been attached to it—horizon being, as the Greek word indicates, a limit from which I pre-comprehend the future. I wait for it. I predetermine it. And thus, I annul it.[164]

Jacques Derrida speaks of the future which is expected, waited for, and predetermined. Such a future is limited, and in this sense it is not a future, or as Derrida would say the future is that to come. Limiting the future, reducing it to the realization of the already given, annuls it. If the future is already expected and known, then it is not the future, the very fact of knowing it cancels it. Moreover, horizon implies a convergence, where this point and the future point eventually are confounded, rendering nothing new whatsoever in the future, but a destitute repetition of semblance. In this regard, the future is defined as what is to come:

> There are two words for "future" in French, which cannot be adequately rendered in English: *futur* and *avenir*. *Futur* stands for "future" as the continuation of the present, as the full actualization of tendencies already in existence; while *avenir* points more towards a radical break, a discontinuity with the present—*avenir* is what is to come (*a venir*), not just what will be. Say, in today's apocalyptic global situation, the ultimate horizon of the future is what Jean-Pierre Dupuy calls the dystopian "fixed point," the zero-point of the ecological breakdown, of global economic and social chaos—even if it is indefinitely postponed, this zero-point is the virtual "attractor" towards which our reality, left to itself, tends.[165]

The distinction between the two words is crucial, and it is the latter future (*avenir*) which holds pertinence to my argument, whatever will come after should not be the former future (*futur*).

> *"The future is inevitable and precise, but it may not occur."*
>
> — Jorge Luis Borges, *La creacin y P.H. Gosse*

Derrida, Heidegger, Passage and Threshold Moment

This starts with Derrida, where future is freed from horizon, the limit of expected convergence. It continues by way of Heidegger, where instead of limits and horizons we have thresholds, a point of entry, the interpenetration of inside and outside, rather than an end point.

In his essay *Building, Dwelling, Thinking*, Heidegger explores the notion of the threshold. His starting premise is the known definition of threshold as the entrance, the doorway, the starting point which opens up unto the architectural space. Heidegger, however, expands the notion beyond its traditional model of mere passage:

> The threshold is the ground-beam that bears the doorway as a whole. It sustains the middle in which the two, the outside and the inside, penetrate each other. The threshold bears the between. What goes out and what goes in, in the between, is joined in the between's dependability.[166]

Heidegger clearly asserts threshold as the ground of the structure, that which holds the inside and the outside thus sustaining them. Threshold becomes the between. [167]

Is this aspect of threshold not akin to the Deleuzean event, an "as-patial" space (and here I refer to both time and space, since according to Heidegger time is a spacing of sorts) not inside or outside but exactly the between which interpenetrates and actualizes both? In other words, it is by way of passing the threshold that inside and outside are differentiated. Threshold is what sustains the being of becoming inside or outside. I will now apply the same rationalization to what I am calling "a threshold moment". In order to elaborate more on this moment, I give the example of Arvo Pärt's Für Alina, a musical piece full of threshold moments.

Pärt composed and performed this piece as part of his newly revealed style of composition, what he refers to as "tintinnabuli"[168], which he introduced in Tallinn in 1976.

The composition appears to be rather simple at first sight, to the extent that anybody willing to spend some time with it may be able to play it. However, the piece is far from simplicity.

Pärt wrote the piece with purity of sound in mind, its interpretation and performance requires an *actualization* of a perfect balance between harmony and symmetry drawn from both the natural acoustics of the piano instrument and the performer.

The score is minimal; it occupies the space of two pages. The notes are a combination of stemless and whole notes, it is bereft of time signatures, except for a tempo marking that reads: "*Ruhig, erhaben, in sich hineinhorchend,*" (peacefully, in an elevated and introspective manner). Any rendition of the piece is imperative in demanding patience and a skilled touch, the notes have to resonate just enough, and be resisted as much, when they are not played.

Für Alina is made of fifteen bars in total. The first bar opens with a pair of impractical B, forming a low double-octave sound, which resonates throughout the entire performance, except for the last section. "Bar number two has one stemless note and one whole note, bar number three has two quarter notes and a whole note, bar number four contains three quarter notes, and a whole note. This pattern continues until a bar with eight notes in total, seven quarter notes and one whole note. From here on it descends back toward two quarter notes and a half note."[169] Succinctly put, bar one has one note, bar two has two notes, bar three has three notes, and so on and so forth. When played softly, and with much composure, leaving time for the notes to resonate, the piece brings forth the immanent dissonance of the piano apparatus.

These first notes form a threshold moment, the doorway into the piece. Moreover, they are what sustain the entire piece in the Heideggerian sense, pedaled, they resonate as the background for the entire work. For Heidegger, threshold names the "between" which bears together as it bears apart, this "between" is the difference.

In a master class, Pärt is asked about *Alina*, he proceeds to play the beginning as he explains:

> "I imagine the conductor having an upbeat. When the whole thing starts we can't hear anything yet. And the people in the concert hall don't know what is coming.
>
> Then the conductor makes the upbeat. The upbeat, the moment when he raises his hand, actually contains the formula of the entire work, its character, dynamics, tempo, and plenty of other things. The conductor and the musicians know it from practicing together."[170]

Those resonating low double octaves, a repetition of difference, a moment announcing the work, the conductor and the performer know the upbeat, this threshold moment, which unfolds perfectly with the opening, sustained B, a repetition with difference. The entire work blossoms, comes out, emerges from within this difference. A moment from which each bar from there on is defined, actualized, and brought into being. In this regard, the threshold is a moment of ecstasies, whence the piece with its notes "become". This is a moment of true *poïesis*, the actualization, the intensive process of pure becoming, the emergence of the new:

> How does actualization occur in things themselves?...Beneath the actual qualities and extensities [of things themselves] there are spatio-temporal dynamisms. They must be surveyed in every domain, even though they are ordinarily hidden by the constituted qualities and extensities.[171]

This process of actualization clearly involves active forces informed by the spontaneity of temporal decisions taken by the performer in this case, as a corollary of performing in *rubato*. And this is further activated by the multiplicities brought forth through the repeated bars. It is the state of minimal difference, the dissonance and the sonorities which take shape out of the interaction, or to be more precise, the interpenetration of the two melodic phrases by means of the threshold moment, the first note. The quixotic B octaves act as "attractors" for the entire process of becoming.

The first phrase is performed by the left hand, alternately supplemented with the second phrase of the right. It is crucial to add that what is not played is as important, if not more, than what is played. This is evident in the typography of the two pages. Pärt is inclined to "write" the white space, which only enhances the stemless note-heads. Everything one needs to know about this piece is found on those pages granted it is read the way it is meant to be, as Pärt intended it.He indicates the threshold, and the process of becoming right in these pages.

When referring to the two phrases, he characterizes them as quite neutral, but both together they blossom, they are brought forth sustained by the threshold: "I had a need to concentrate on each sound so that every blade of grass would be as important as a flower...as if they last an entire life, or future or past, outside time...its not the tune that matters so much here, it is the combination, its makes such a heart-rendering union, the soul yearns to sing it endlessly."[172]

The two phrases are not in direct relation to one another, Pärt draws this relationship as analogous to "two people whose paths seem to cross but they don't."[173] In order for them to 'make sense', they have to be connected via the virtual field, which is precisely those white spaces, the absences, that which is not played. This process is referenced in the typography, right in these pages, it is something of an *Augenmusik*, Pärt accounts for this absence visually on the score sheet. The absence of a time signature is ineluctably freeing, yet introspective of both the performer and the listener; one has to respond to the notes, and the occasional dissonance that emerges from the simultaneity of both moments.

Only the proper performer is apt to play the existing notes so that one would be able to listen or actually feel what is equally important and "there" but is not played, the virtual continuum, where the process of pure differentiation of the two moments occur.

This is exactly what renders this progression tend towards the infinite, as one ought to think of *Für Alina* threshold moment as a creative activity, one that namely creates time-space. It presents us with the present, one that is filled up with the actualization of the pure past, and the anticipation of the future. It is a moment of eternal return.

Interestingly enough Pärt's *Tintinnabuli*, can be expounded as "the application of various inversions of a certain chord. Also, it is a word which evokes the pealing of bells, the bells' complex but rich sonorous mass of overtones, the gradual unfolding of patterns implicit in the sound itself, and the idea of a sound that is simultaneously static and in flux,"[174] this description is one worthy of the Deleuzean plane of immanence or the virtual field, or as Pärt explains it:

> Tintinnabulation is an area I sometimes wander into when I am searching for answers—in my life, my music, my work. In my dark hours, I have the certain feeling that everything outside this one thing has no meaning. Traces of this perfect thing appear in many guises—and everything that is unimportant falls away. Tintinnabulation is like this. . . . [175]

Moreover, Pärt's strong religious feeling is mirrored in his attempts to bring forth what is unknowable, and this characterizes his work, especially the *Tintinnabuli* with a deep *nouminal* aspect. Consequently, as with *Für Alina,* Pärt's music transports the listener to a moment outside time, an atemporality, which emerges from the silence, the pure difference that begins the work, and which he always returns to throughout as the structure of the work itself.

The word trace should be highlighted here. Pärt's use of the term is rather close to what Derrida means or at least alludes to: a mark of the absence of a presence, an always-already absent present, the virtual background of differentiation, that which brings forth the actualization of the Idea. In retrospect, this trace is what Žižek posits as "unfathomable X", or what both Derrida and Samuel Beckett agree on calling *l'innommable*, the unnamable, a moment of positive, creative, affirmative experience of difference. In other words, it is that which opens up unto the universal, the Idea.

As a result, it is only fitting to conclude this section with the words of Samuel Beckett filling up the white space of the paper, a threshold that sustains the entire structure of my argument thus far:

> Je suis ce cours de sable qui glisse
> entre le galet et la dune
> la pluie d'été pleut sur ma vie
> sur moi ma vie qui me fuit me poursuit
> et finira le jour de son commencement
>
> cher instant je te vois
> dans ce rideau de brume qui recule
> où je n'aurai plus à fouler ces longs seuils mouvants
> et vivrai le temps d'une porte
> qui s'ouvre et se referme
>
> my way is in the sand flowing
> between the shingle and the dune
> the summer rain rains on my life
> on me my life harrying fleeing
> to its beginning to its end
>
> my peace is there in the receding mist
> when I may cease from treading these long shifting thresholds
> and live the space of a door
> that opens and shuts[176]

"Time is the Mind of Space."

— Samuel Alexander, Space, *Time and Deity*

"Beyond the edge of the world there's a space where emptiness and substance neatly overlap, where past and future form a continuous. And, hovering about, there are signs no one has ever read, chords no one has ever heard."

— Haruki Murakami, *Kafka on the Shore*

7. Revolutionary Spacing

At the beginning of this part, the spirit of the last section is carried still, as a supplement, or more precisely a continuity, one that sustains as it progresses. And perhaps it is best for another poet to lead through.

In *Species of Spaces and Other pieces*, Georges Perec writes:

> "This is how space begins, with words only, signs traced on the blank page. To describe space: to name it, to trace it, like those portolano-makers who saturated the coastlines with the names of harbours, the names of capes, the names of inlets, until in the end the land was only separated from the sea by a continuous ribbon of text." [177]

It starts perfectly with signs traced, signs of the problematic Idea, that are differentiated, re-actualized, a spacing not as emptying out that which is already spatial, but filling it with virtualities that become actual. Moving from a threshold moment, an atemporal moment, which sustains becoming, to the space which is filled with such a threshold, or as Beckett puts it the "space of a door which opens and shuts". [178]

In-Between Space: Place as Passage, from Derrida to Anarchitecture

Gordon Matta-Clark is adamant to point out that the threshold is always site specific. In my argument, this translates as the fact that no such threshold moment can ever exist, without the spacing for it. Such spacing is created by the revolution, it is a spacing, making room for a place.

Matta-Clark is primarily concerned with investigating places "extra architecture", as these places exhibit an attempt to de-rationalize space, to render space unfathomable, as something that resists symbolization and eventually, identity and semblance. Matta-Clark's premise is to deprive the structure itself of any fixed point that could reduce the space or represent it in terms of its underlying structure. It is vital to allude to what Derrida has to say about threshold in *The Post Card: From Socrates to Freud and Beyond.* Derrida demonstrates the inability of threshold as a material entity to "hold itself":

> "The place is only a place of passage, and more precisely, a threshold. But a threshold, this time, to give access to what is no longer a place. A subordination, a relativisation of the place, and an extraordinary consequence; the place is Being. What finds itself reduced to the condition of a threshold is Being itself, Being as place." [179]

For Derrida the threshold is also, then, conceptually, a place of emanation, of becoming.This is prominent in Gordon Matta-Clark's work, especially where he contrasts the living room and the street, the outside and the inside. Matta-Clark through differentiation, redefines both the "inside" and "outside", thus reinterpreting their given architecture.

Matta-Clark writes:

> What we understand as building, or see as the urban landscape is just this sort of middle zone, that given ingredient which is somewhat useful and obedient. But is really just the beginning of speculations about what could be beyond it and what numbers of direction there could be.[180]

The threshold moment is sustained, held in place by the spatial opening that the revolution creates. This threshold is twofold then, the first is atemporal, whereas the second is spatial. The first is a moment of eternity in the present, where past and future are sustained, interpenetrated by means of this endless present. The second differentiates, it re-actualizes, brings forth, through "leaking" the virtual force of the Idea, the emergence of the radically new.

Differential Unity: the Idea and Heidegger's Fourfold

At the beginning of this part, I mentioned the sustaining continuity, that which leads through. I will now refer to it as a bridge, in the Heideggerian sense of the term:

> The bridge swings over the stream with case and power. It does not just connect banks that are already there. The banks emerge as banks only as the bridge crosses the stream. The bridge designedly causes them to lie across from each other. One side is set off against the other by the bridge. Nor do the banks stretch along the stream as indifferent border strips of the dry land. With the banks, the bridge brings to the stream the one and the other expanse of the landscape lying behind them. It brings stream and bank and land into each other's neighborhood. The bridge *gathers* the earth as landscape around the stream. Thus it guides and attends the stream through the meadows. Resting upright in the stream's bed, the bridge-piers bear the swing of the arches that leave the stream's waters to run their course. The waters may wander on quiet and gay, the sky's floods from storm or thaw may shoot past the piers in torrential waves—the bridge is ready for the sky's weather and its fickle nature. Even where the bridge covers the stream, it holds its flow up to the sky by taking it for a moment under the vaulted gateway and then setting it free once more. [181]

The bridge for Heidegger sustains as it brings forth, and in this sense it is my notion of the spatial threshold, that which leads and enables becoming. Heidegger suggests that the banks emerge as banks only due to the bridge, they are actualized as what lies across of one another. Moreover, the bridge allows for the water to flow, for what is vital to be brought forth, the flow is held for a moment before it is set free, as Heidegger puts it. It is this description that I attribute to my understanding of the revolutionary spacing. Where first I have introduced the time-space of revolution, that threshold moment which opens unto eternity, here I assign to that mindfulness its actualization, or what enables the experience of such a moment. The image of the bridge which Heidegger perfectly illustrates, is more than appropriate when it comes to designating such a spacing. Additionally, when Heidegger speaks of the duly gathering nature of the bridge, he points out to the fact that a bridge differentiates as it leads, or creates passage. Consequently, Heidegger suggests that in its gathering the bridge allows a site for what he calls *fourfold* or *Geviert*.

Geviert is a phenomenon that stems out from an immanence of the unity of four perspectives: earth, sky, divinites, and mortals. This notion is poetic, as it is featured in Hölderlin.

Neither of the four perspectives is considered on its own, immanently at once. *Geviert* or its English counterpart Fourfold, which is present in Heidegger is a clear Kierkegaardian "leap", from negation, and its sublation, or the Hegelian dialectic thinking. This leap is capable of thinking difference as such, it does not relegate all four perspectives to semblance or identity, but posits a location where all four occur at once. Since these perspectives are non philosophical terms, but rather poetic as Wolfgang Schirmacher points out,[182] I will be approaching their "differential" unity accordingly. My first approach is that of the word itself, specifically that which is the origin, the *Aleph*. My second is by way of architecture, or what Gaston Bachelard calls the *poetics of space*. As for my third, it is mathematical, what for Einstein is the poetry of logic. To conclude, I will come to a synthesis of all three.

My discussion of *Geviert* should not be misunderstood as a deviation, but as a conversation[183] of revolutionary *spacing,* which eventually will "gather" the various aspects of my intent. I will be communicating *Geviert* as singularity. In addition, my conversation will be corollary to the following quote:

> But only something *that is itself a location* can make space for a site. The location is not already there before the bridge is. Before the bridge stands, there are of course many spots along the stream that can be occupied by something. One of them proves to be a location, and does so *because of the bridge.* Thus the bridge does not first come to a location to stand in it; rather, a location comes into existence only by virtue of the bridge. The bridge is a thing; it gathers the fourfold, but in such a way that it allows a site for the fourfold. By this site are determined the localities and ways by which a space is provided for. [184]

Explosion of the Real: the site for Borges's Aleph and the Limits of Language

Beatriz Viterbo has died, and on that same day, Jorge Luis Borges noticed the advertisement billboards around Constitution Plaza were being changed. This change urges him to think of his own, and to resolutely stand against the ever-changing universe. He will forevermore hold and cherish every single memory and image he has of Beatriz.

In order to do so, he supposes an annual visit to Beatriz's family house is due, as an act of devotion and in paying respects to her memory. Borges chooses the thirtieth of April as the assigned date for his annual visit, which so happens to be Beatriz's birthday. Every year, her memory is revitalized with every visit Borges recollects and repeats at the same time. He carefully relives all those past moments the two have spent together, as he turns to the photos of Beatriz found all around the house with new insights and conversations.

Borges is faithful to his annual resolution, but he finds himself every year arriving later than he did on his initial visit, which was at 7:15, and every year staying a bit longer.Within the space of the house, Borges converses mostly with Beatriz's first cousin, Carlos Argentino Daneri, a self proclaimed poet, who according to Borges was more full of himself than being poetically insightful.

With time, Borges gains the confidence of Daneri, who in turn starts sharing some of his poetry with the former.

On one occasion, Daneri calls on Borges proposing they both meet at a salon bar right next door to Beatriz's family house, that is owned and run by the landlords of the house, Zunino and Zungri.

At their meeting, Daneri rereads to Borges five different excerpts which the narrator is already familiar with. However, they seemed different having undergone some sort of verbal ostentation.

By the end of the rereading, Daneri informs Borges of his intention to publish his initial cantos. Daneri adds that the reason he called upon Borges to meet with him for some cocktails is to ask him for a favor. Daneri would like nothing more than to have the prestigious writer and poet Álvaro Melián Lafinur to write some opening words for Daneri's publication.

As the days passed, Borges dismissed Daneri's request, driven by his contempt to both Carlos Argentino and his poetry, but within him there was a fear that Daneri would call him incessantly as to inquire about it. Nevertheless, time passed until one day a distressed Carlos calls Borges only to reveal his state is solely due to the fact that his landlords, Zunino and Zungri, have plans to demolish Beatriz's family house, under the pretence of expanding the already oversized salon bar.

Daneri attributes his distraught to the fact that he can only finish his poem (his life work) in the space of the house, since down in the very darkness of the cellar there exists an *Aleph*; that which sustains and gathers as a space all other spaces:

> It's in the cellar under the dining room…It's mine — mine. I discovered it when I was a child, all by myself. The cellar stairway is so steep that my aunt and uncle forbade my using it, but I'd heard someone say there was a world down there. I found out later they meant an old-fashioned globe of the world, but at the time I thought they were referring to the world itself. One day when no one was home I started down in secret, but I stumbled and fell. When I opened my eyes, I saw the *Aleph*…. Yes, the only place on earth where all places are — seen from every angle, each standing clear, without any confusion or blending. I kept the discovery to myself and went back every chance I got. As a child, I did not foresee that this privilege was granted me so that later I could write the poem. Zunino and Zungri will not strip me of what's mine — no, and a thousand times no![185]

Borges hastily comes over, for he wants to see the *Aleph* for himself, afterall he needs to examine this *Aleph* to believe in it, and in doing so Borges is not one to take a "leap".

Upon Borges's arrival to the family house on Garay Street, Daneri instructs him that in order to see the *Aleph* one has to lie flat on one's back in utter stillness, as one focuses both eyes from that position on the floor, on the nineteenth step. Daneri soon leaves the cellar as he turns off the lights and closes the trapdoor.

For a moment Borges is overcome with fear, thinking that in order to conceal his mad inclination and his spitefulness, since Borges has not contacted Lafinur with what Carlos has previously requested, Daneri has devised this whole *Aleph* thing simply to lure him into the dark confines of the cellar and to trap him there to his death.

But to Borges's relief and utter amazement, after a minute or two, he sees the *Aleph*:

> I arrive now at the ineffable core of my story. And here begins my despair as a writer. All language is a set of symbols whose use among its speakers assumes a shared past. How, then, can I trans-

> late into words the limitless *Aleph*, which my floundering mind can scarcely encompass? Mystics, faced with the same problem, fall back on symbols: to signify the godhead, one Persian speaks of a bird that somehow is all birds; Alanus de Insulis, of a sphere whose center is everywhere and circumference is nowhere; Ezekiel, of a four-faced angel who at one and the same time moves east and west, north and south (Not in vain do I recall these inconceivable analogies; they bear some relation to the *Aleph*).
> Perhaps the gods might grant me a similar metaphor, but then this account would become contaminated by literature, by fiction. Really, what I want to do is impossible, for any listing of an endless series is doomed to be infinitesimal. In that single gigantic instant I saw millions of acts both delightful and awful; not one of them occupied the same point in space, without overlapping or transparency. What my eyes beheld was simultaneous, but what I shall now write down will be successive, because language is successive. Nonetheless, I'll try to recollect what I can.[186]

Borges asserts the unnamable, that which is infinitesimally different but at the same time occupying the same point in space. Is this point which resists symbolizations, and cannot be represented with symbolic language not Heidegger's *Geviert*? Precisely that which opens first of all, then "bridges" between the "here" and "there", and in doing so sustains both as it gathers earth and sky, divinities and mortals.

In the concluding remarks to *El Aleph*, Borges affirms this gathering as passage in his reference to the *Kabalistic Aleph*. He notes the *Aleph* as the prime letter of the proto-Canaanite alphabet, and its shape is that of a man, whilst grounded on earth, is pointing upwards towards the sky. Moreover, man could be understood in this context, as the twofold of divinities and mortals.

Within the space of language, its confines and its limits, I have come to briefly deal with the fourfolds to present that point which contains all other points. I guess it is better left to Borges and poetry to reveal what I might not be able to do with plain words, to instill the sensation of that point. I believe Gaston Bachelard formulates it best when he writes:

> Words ... are little houses, each with its cellar and garret. Common sense lives on the ground floor, always ready to engage in 'foreign

> commerce' on the same level as the others, as the passers-by, who are never dreamers. To go upstairs in the word house is to withdraw step by step; while to go down to the cellar is to dream, it is losing oneself in the distant corridors of an obscure etymology, looking for treasures that cannot be found in words. To mount and descend in the words themselves—this is a poet's life. To mount too high or descend too low is allowed in the case of poets, who bring earth and sky together.[187]

The *Aleph* down in the cellar of the house of Garay Street is exactly that treasure which words fail to find.

Additionally, I return to the excerpt from Heidegger, the one which I declared to be the premise of my discussion. It is through this quote that I am able to explain this. And so, I repeat:

> But only something *that is itself a location* can make space for a site. The location is not already there before the bridge is. Before the bridge stands, there are of course many spots along the stream that can be occupied by something. One of them proves to be a location, and does so *because of the bridge.* Thus the bridge does not first come to a location to stand in it; rather, a location comes into existence only by virtue of the bridge. The bridge is a thing; it gathers the fourfold, but in such a way that it allows a site for the fourfold. By this site are determined the localities and ways by which a space is provided for.[188]

The *Aleph* occupies a certain point in space. The steep staircase leading down to the cellar makes the *spacing* for that point. The young Carlos was thrown (*geworfen*) into this space and as a result, it became a location for him, one that contains a world. There is evidence of this throwness (*geworfenheit*) in the short novel, where Borges "saw millions of acts delightful and awful."[189] Both Daneri and Borges are not bound by their past, they do perceive it as they perceive the infinite all in the *Aleph*, like a plane of immanence; there is no without, all is contained in that point, or plane, and in the *Aleph* they are free. This freedom is fashioned into existence only by the threshold (the latter definition, the spacing), and one ought to read revolutionary spacing in exactly those terms.

A crucial remark is to be made here, Daneri in his explanation of the process, tells Borges that if he were to miss the *Aleph*, Borges's incapacity does not annul Carlos' experience.

This is simply a reiteration, or a verbal variation of the Kantian enthusiasm, which Deleuze delineates as that with which the revolutionary Idea is thought within the plane of immanence. It clears all the historical limitations and conditions, which restrict immanence. Borges has refused to go on. He has built for himself a metaphorical prison, where he has conveniently locked himself with all the memories of Beatriz. This state that he "dwells" in is past, a withdrawal from the life-world, and in the Heideggerian sense he has lost his freedom.The only way to regain it is to be thrown, in such a way as to consider the past, and alternately the present, not as deterministic, but to redefine both towards an open ended future.

It is only after Borges experiences the *Aleph* for himself that he encourages Carlos to allow the demolition of the family house. Moreover, Borges came face to face with the "real thing". Whence he was inside his constructs of the past, the safety of his familiarities, as soon as he looked into the *Aleph*, the Real exploded right in his face, thus bringing him to experience things beyond his grasp or capacity. Borges wants to retreat back into the Symbolic order, where he is apt to delineate himself and the world around him through language and the familiar.

Borges writes of a lack, the lack of the ineffability of the *Aleph*. His experience of it allows him to see all things from varying perspectives at all times, yet at the same time hindering his expression or representation of it.

On this note, and in returning to poetic sensations, a passage:

"I should say: the house shelters day-dreaming, the house protects the dreamer, the house allows one to dream in peace."

— Gaston Bachelard, *The Poetics of Space*

Phenomenology of Architecture: Schirmacher's City as Geviert

Wolfgang Schirmacher borrows from grammar the technical term "sentence structure", only to extrapolate it into a convenient metaphor designating the link between language and architecture. His approach lies in the Spirit of Heidegger's title of *Building Dwelling Thinking*, in this regard Schirmacher asserts architecture as the poetics of dwelling.

For Schirmacher, combining Heidegger's thinking of language with urbanism is crucial for the formulation of an architectural philosophy, one that is supplemented by some practical notion, or to be more precise, what is missing still for Schirmacher, is a comprehensive point of view to elevate building to the level of thinking. Schirmacher provides a solution to this problem, as he locates in Holderlin's *Geviert* both a theoretical and practical novelty. He coins this approach, the city as *Geviert*, or the fourfolds for Heidegger. *Geviert* theory/praxis enables a retreat from the transcendental, and a return to the immanent lifeworld. Moreover, *Geviert* is lived intuition, a holistic experience, an imperturbable intuition, which is simultaneously emotional, intellectual, physical, and social. *Geviert* is by no means utopian, as alternately both an aesthetico-ethical experience and an authentic language activity; it is inconspicuous as the persistent possibility of being, closely accessible, however remaining as the median of the lack of language.

The four perspectives, dimensions, aspects of *Geviert* (the earth, the sky, divinities and mortals) need each other and are always untrue if individualized. Schirmacher explains that each of the separate dimensions have been thought of and theorized, but there has never been any theory approaching or laying down the thinking and practice of their "differential unity".

According to Schirmacher, the city as *Geviert* is first and foremost the site for the theory and praxis of the metropolis. For Plato, knowledge of the truth and city life are inextricable, i.e. city life—and for Heidegger dwelling—coupled with philosophy, they both bring forth the foundation for the political, which constitutes the unity of the city, the differential unity, the metropolis.

Phenomenologically, Schirmacher remarks that due to postmodernism, cities are swiftly depopulating at the center, as opposed to their peripheries or outskirts, which are proliferating like a viral infestation. Furthermore, these postmodern cities are characterized by dispersal, decentralization, loosening, which tears apart the shimmering "skin of the city", making way to a mood of fear, anxiety, and boredom. The city is broken up into suburbs, the scattered unplanned chaos. Poets are mourning their cultural motherland, the streets, where as flaneurs they walked and wandered, and consequently thought and created. Respect for differences, which is at the foundation of the metropolis or the city space, is tranformed into contempt: a confrontation between rich and poor. Public area and pedestrian zones are relegated to the daily backdrop of shopping and business.

At this stage, a vital question emerges; how can the metropolis be restored? Or to ask it in more relevant terms, what makes the city space a city? Or as Heidegger would say, what makes the city space a place, as location that gathers the fourfold?

Schirmacher asserts that city planning and building in the manner of the fourfold can be achieved, however it is ineluctable to rid both of the simplistic attitude of consumerism, and the process of autocratic planning and standardized manufacturing.

Internal change is imperative for the emergence of a fourfold praxis. Although cities are becoming inhospitable, there exists no other alternative to them as a place of dwelling/residence. Some attempts at the fourfold thinking/praxis can be already acknowledged.

The work of Gordon Matta-Clark brings forth a *Geviert* theory/praxis. In what follows, I will pragmatically describe Schirmacher's approach to the city and building as fourfold.

First, I start with a quote taken from an audio interview, where Matta-Clark says something very similar to the notion of the fourfold. Matta-Clark in answering his interviewer, concerning how he experiences his work, says:

> The sort of space that can involve yourself in…that you could go through it. You had to feel the things you made… every point could be different, and when you went through it, to firm up… a global idea, and this global idea of feeling, I don't know how to call it… Well, literally a global form of some sorts…of having to relate to the details on the inside in such a way that you would reconstruct

> that global form. And the only way to have a percepetion of it is experience.[190]

Matta-Clark is unknowingly describing the fourfold, for him it is that unnamable, that which is only experienced, he cannot fully express it in words.

As the interview proceeds, Matta-Clark is asked about the spacing and what might his current or future projects be. He begins first off with speaking about the opening up of space, or what he coins as the flexibility in experiencing the space, as opposed to the historical conformity and favoring of rigid architectural structures.

Matta-Clark elucidates to the domestic environment, where under the standardized commercial driven building plans of postmodern cities, "we have this cellular repetition, this sort of modular thinking."[191] This urban context lacks any transitional or shared spaces, and if they do exist, they are "highly limited and unanimated." [192] At this moment in the interview, Matta-Clark is very close to Schirmacher as he talks about pedestrian-oriented zones, which are relegated in the postmodern city to a "plaza" like pedestrian mall, where the place of dwelling and wandering becomes a daily backdrop to the commercial activities, and similarly the stores mimic various kinds of street life, but as soon as darkness falls and the stores are closed these spaces are void and scary.

Matta-Clark emphasizes the idea of how to animate, share, and create a space. Furthermore, he maintains that making something happen is to restate the problem. Creating central spaces as an idea has always been there, and people have always had the need for some space or forum. However, the idea does not happen largely due to the large commercialized consumer oriented building. Most downtown areas, where a forum is supposed to be, "has become a real urban situation, sure then people will pass through it and they will sit in it on a sunny day, but it doesn't have anything to do with people sharing very much of anything – it's just a space." [193]

There exists a possibility for creating spaces in an urban high-rise, given that the people are all working together, which proves to be a vital part, where they have something in common, a shared trait, or characteristic. This might be their shared sense of belonging to the building, or their experience of owning the space, or that the building instills in them a certain identity, or simply that they all shared in making it. Starting from this premise, it is possible to have some sort of transformation.

During the interview, Matta-Clark contributes the non-existence of such shared experienced spaces, those that form an essential part of the metropolis, and which would enable us to achieve a fourfold praxis, to economics, building and real estate value. Once the economic situation is altered, prices have decreased and market value has fallen, some range of experimentation would be possible, something that never existed "before, it is sort of like: as the old, complete exploiting economy disintegrates, some kind of new idea can rise out of it…the idea of always going somewhere new rather than just rebuilding the old: I think that's really the process."[194] His approach is artistic, as he explains, and artistic activities have more to do with point in a certain way, "a way of looking or a way of thinking." [195] His involvement is with creating spatial perceptions, or events.

It is not suprising that Matta-Clark made use of the camera throughout his work. At first it was simply applied as a recording device that documented his artistic process, but soon enough it was deployed as a viable apparatus for perceiving architectural, urban, and social space.

Assisting in capturing spatial disorientations and his infamous structural interventions, the camera filled in for the lack of language, in experiencing and sharing both the spatial and the ineffable in his theory and praxis. One could say that by means of the camera, the fourfold approach of Gordon Matta-Clark was revealed.

The camera aptly navigated the building cuts revealing weight, movement, depth, sensation of the space, reallocation of light, the temporality (the camera presenting the viewer with the nomadic time)[196], and the interpenetration of inside and outside, or the "here" and "there", by the cut, or the intervention.

Additionally, the camera moves as free as the liberating spaces, which Matta-Clark introduces, it could go in all direction, and could see from all perspectives.

Matta-Clark surpasses anchored vision, which is somewhat obsolete and redundant. He presents instead a reception of the world as is, freed from the shackles of representation, semblance, and historicism. It is in this regard that Matta-Clark liberates not only the space, and by doing so he is also liberating perception and experience from historical context, and its inability to reinvent the world, or for the radically new to emerge due to the adherence or the projection of any given experience onto the past, as a historical interpretation.

In other words, what he is urging us to do is not to make sense or read these spatial events, or the spatio-perceptive experience with "certain vocabularies" [197] which he finds "completely archaic and basically impoverished, but in a completely radically new spatial vocabulary, or spatial techniques, which can then be applied to a number of things." [198]

The liberating spatial perception is corollary in allowing for a holistic experience and vision of the world, and with doing away with any fixed concrete interpretation, it is as if Gordon Matta Clark is escorting us right into the cellar, asking us to follow certain attractors and to adjust our perception, and once we do so we will see the *Aleph*.

Additionally, Matta-Clark speaks of spatial attitudes:

> The reason I deal with cities, the reason I deal with architecture because I think that there are many things that can be and should be played with, remodified or reconsidered in that process. *central for me is how to go through space, how to feel space, how to recreate a space.* And how to liberate space. And liberating space means… Say, in the past project for me, liberating space meant transforming a certain kind of conventional enclosure into something where, if nothing else, light and air pass through it. The other implications, or the ones that are much harder to justify, that the spatial attitude can then be projected into the urban experience in a variety of ways, and with far more extensive meanings.
>
> It's kind of an ambition of mine to make the global space and to give it a social integration. Well it would fantastic to get to the next stage, which seems to me to be working with people who would experience it. [199]

Being within a closed space, one always seems to experience the outside space through a window or a screen of some sort, as if the outside is an artificial image, not quite real by the inside standards. When one opens a window or steps outside on a balcony or porch, or terrace, there is a shocking feeling of a direct proximity, as if one never expected the outside to be "here."

By opening up, or cutting, Matta-Clark is removing this distinction between outside and inside, but this should not be understood as simply bridging the gap between both states, rather what Matta-Clark's work enables is the emergence of the third space, which is the result of such an encroaching, one that encompasses all the spaces possible, the point of *Geviert*.

Schirmacher and Matta-Clark: Towards a Praxis of Geviert

Matta-Clark speaks of vocabulary and attitudes, alternately, Schirmacher highlights the amalgamation of sentence structure, and city planning and building. *Geviert* persists in both, one laying down the theoretical foundation and plotting it as the architectural blueprint,while the other via splitting, cutting, and opening up, renders it a spatial praxis. "A philosophy of architecture will emphasize the artistic character of the building, the model of the 'master builder' will not follow the example of the 'divine creator', nor will building follow personal taste, and consumerist needs, That is the path of architecture unto the fourfold."[200]

The architect or the builder has to be equipped with a particular attitude, one where he sees the whole world from every single perspective, and in liberating spaces, is able to sustain the openness of the space, or of spacing the space (*Einräumen*). *Geviert* praxis is only achieved by a change in attitude supplemented by new spatial vocabularies, recognizing the question put forth by city life, and the lifeworld.

=Žižek alludes to a similar proposition, where he posits an attitude that enables the perception of the opening up, or the liberating of space: the parallax. He borrows this attitude from Kojin Karatani. Žižek explains the parallax to be "the apparent displacement of an object (the shift of position against a background), caused by a change in observational position that provides a new line of sight. The philosophical twist to be added, of course, is that the observed difference is not simply 'subjective' due to the fact that the same object which exists 'out there' is seen from two different stances, or the point of view. It is rather that, as Hegel would have put it, subject and object are inherently 'mediated', so that an 'epistemological' shift in the subject's point of view always reflects an 'ontological' shift in the object itself."[201]

In an attempt to answer the deadlock of social antagonism, Žižek turns to architecture. He contends that building, as a space, provides an answer to class struggle. It is by way of the parallax that the third place, which is opened up by the amalgamation of inside and outside, as with the work of Matta-Clark, the virtual space (or plane of immanence) emerges, as the creative artistic moment, where new emerges.

Additionally, Žižek asserts that the architectural parallax inscribes the changing temporal experience within the space itself, where it is "a little bit like a cubist painting, presenting the same object from different perspectives, condensing into the same spatial surface a temporal extension. Through the parallax gap in the object itself, 'time becomes space'... The task is, to conceive of all possible positions as responses to a certain underlying deadlock or antagonism, as so many attempts to resolve this deadlock."[202]

Consequently, Žižek proposes what would constitute his 'dream house': a place which is strictly made up of secondary spaces, and places of passage; staircase, corridors, storage rooms, kitchen, bathrooms, but no sitting room or bedroom;[203] Žižek's dream is to inhabit Heidegger's bridge.

This bridge however, as Heidegger suggests, is the location that makes space for the site of the fourfold. Applied to the city, Žižek's dream space corresponds to what Deleuze calls "disjunctive synthesis"[204], the production of differences. The city becomes that point, which incorporates all points, from all different perspectives, where difference unfolds, an open ended disjunction of connected liberated differentiation.

The following is an account of a historical situation, the deadlock of social antagonism, related to the architectural motif. I present this case as the obverse of the *fourfolds* in architecture; however sadly, such a deadlock has been the governing rhetoric of mobilizations and uprisings in contemporary times.

Written in 1975, *High-Rise* demonstrates J.G. Ballard's prescience of urban change and social antagonism. The novel takes as its subject matter one out of five identical units in development, as a residential project set in the abandoned area of the London Docklands. The location is two miles away from the center of the city, separating between Nineteenth century terraced houses, and empty factories and forlorn warehouses. The high-rise tower is architecturally and aesthetically isolated, it creates for its tenants a different time and space, providing and catering for their accommodation and comfort: swimming pools, school, supermarket, high-speed elevators, and as such severing any connection with the outside world. Ballard describes the structure as a technological marvel, and accordingly it "frees" its tenants from communal sharing or interaction as it tends to their individual needs, it does not serve the collective whole, or the body of residents.

The building is the first to be completed, it spans forty stories upwards. Shortly after its last property has been occupied, signs of social change begin to be pronounced.

The residents collapse into barbaric primitive hunter/gatherer behavior, where everything starts to break down; people get killed, mobs are formed that raid, steal and destroy, and soon enough everything breaks out of control.

High-Rise presents a characterization of the classes demanding their needs no matter the costs, as was evident in the London riots of 2011. The shoppers were deprived of their individual needs, of the very thing that allows them to shop, and eventually to satisfy their desires. As soon as the varying social levels of the high-rise start facing this handicap (due to some failure to satisfy on behalf of the high-rise itself), they act out against one another, the rejection of this architectural landscape triggers a state of divide, a political line up of "us" versus "them". The failure of architecture and urban structure has its repercussions on the socio-political life; the lack of shared spaces, locations of gathering which liberate the isolated apartment modules of the high-rise breeds hostility, aggression, and a two-sided conflict.

As the narrative unfolds, the building becomes a landscape of anxieties, fear, and boredom.

Within the high-rise "there exists as well a group of bored apartment-bound housewives and stay-at-home adult daughters who spend a large part of their time riding the elevators, and wandering the long corridors…migrating endlessly in search of change or excitement."[205]

Are those not searching for the spaces of Matta-Clark, or trying to catch a glimpse of Žižek 's dream house?

And all of those who are residents of the high-rise "are essentially prisoners of an eventless world of solitary confinement in a social structure nurtured by a machine."[206]

Between the first and the ninth floors, reside the working class, technicians, and air stewardesses. Between the tenth and the thirty-fifth lies middle class territory, and the uppermost five floors house the rich. As the high-rise yields to power failures, elevator breakdowns, littering, acts of violence, and random hostility breaks out between the three classes.

As a consequence, Ballard tells the story from three different perspectives, or the novel deals with the activities of three different characters: Richard Wilder, lower floors tenant, film producer, Dr. Robert Laing, middle class academic, and lastly Anthony Royal, the architect responsible for the creation and construction of the high-rise unit, the engineer of the opportunity for friction.

Wilder attempts to explore the building with his camera in order to make way for some other perspective, rather than the crushing weight of the structure on him, the perspcetive from his lower level apartment. He finds himself, however always already confined, and so is his vision. Perhaps in an unintentional gesture, Ballard assigns to Wilder the task of countering Matta-Clark's *Geviert,* where Wilder is incapacitated by language, its lack to experience that moment, the *Aleph.*

Royal, in attempt to bring order and reign over the building, organizes a mob and eventually in his own attempt to redeem himself and his creation, falls victim to his lack of creating liberated shared spaces within the high-rise, a failed architect by both Schirmacher's and Heidegger's standards. Laing is the only one to survive the violent social outbursts; he adapts, and passively goes by, maybe as a critique to the helplessness of academia in resolving the deadlock or social struggle and antagonism.

A second examination of Matta-Clark's praxis, or a repetition of my approach, imparts a solution to the deadlock present in *High-Rise.*

Matta-Clark had plans for a piece in New York, which involves acquiring tenement buildings, and transforming them into new spaces, an amalgamation of living and gathering spaces, or spaces for the collective. He elaborates on this approach as a mixture of spaces of living and grouping:

> something where people can have... instead of living in an apartment, in a particular closure, they will have their private space, but they will also have some kind of space towards the top, like a big skylight with a space underneath it. Something that transforms the way people use the building. It's more an issue in New York, especially, where people are completely packed in. [207]

There is a genuine lack of spaces where people can meet, and this is the real issue, especially in an urban context, where the varying social classes are located.

Matta-Clark accounts for those who are active in transforming their lives, in sharing more, in looking after one another, those who out of tradition and close family ties have a sense of caring for the community, and their counter part, those who are involved in violent criminal outbursts as a result from their disturbed experience of reality.

Matta-Clark's approach to the tenement buildings, is to take two which are right next to each other, and rethink the whole space they occupy. He is aiming for a collaborative way to make the structure for the building working in tandem with the residents, a collaborative architecture, or space building, one that communicates with the tenants and considers all the perspectives of the lifeworld, rather than some consumerist driven building.

Eventually, there is a moment of truth amongst this Ballardian mayhem. Laing, the only male protagonist to have survived by the end of the novel, seems to be liberated from the deception of the free lifestyle courtesy of the high-rise invidualistic satisfaction and isolation:

> Laing looked out at the high-rise four hundred yards away. A temporary power failure had occurred, and on the 7th floor all the lights were out. Already torch-beams were moving about in the darkness, as the residents made their first confused attempts to discover where they were. Laing watched them contentedly, ready to welcome them to their new world.[208]

Furthermore, at the heart of the novel resides a question, one concerning the nature of freedom, and what it means to live "freely". The tenants all struggled for their own freedom, an isolated selfish desire to fulfill their every need by any means necessary. Is this not the mirror image of what goes on in cities around the world, where freedom is reduced to a self-centered individual act expressed in destructive violence aiming to delete the other?

What should be the case instead is the peaceful freedom of the collective, the universal.

Freedom is not exclusive of anyone, as such it should be considered as a universal enthusiastic attitude.

Space, Singularity, and the Differential

Singularity is an indispensible component of the Deleuzean ontology. Moreover, singularities are key constituents of the haecceity of things. Singularities are not from without, but are strictly immanent. As Deleuze writes:

> There is no abstract universal beyond the individual or beyond the particular and the general: it is singularity itself which is 'pre-individual'. [209]

However, singularities are not qualities, attributes, or characteristics, they are instead that which is within, and generates qualities, and shapes, under a given force field:

> singularities are turning points and points of inflection; bottlenecks, knots, foyers, and centers; points of fusion and condensation, and boiling; points of tears and joy, sickness and health, hope and anxiety, 'sensitive' points.[210]

Here, Deleuze defines singularities as points of tension where unpredictability occurs, therefore one can designate the Deleuzean singularity as the site of the revolutionary.

Deleuze and Guattari in *A Thousand Plateaus* allude to the unpredictability of singularities:

> On the one hand, to the formed or formable matter we must add an entire energetic materiality in movement, carrying singularities or **haecceities** that are already like implicit forms that are topological, rather than geometrical, and that combine with processes of deformation: for example, the variable undulations and torsions of the fibers guiding the operation of splitting wood. On the other hand, to the essential properties of matter deriving from the formal essence we must add **variable intensive affects**, now resulting from the operation, now on the contrary making possible: for example, wood that is more or less porous, more or less elastic and resistant. At any rate, it is a question of surrendering to the wood, then following where it leads by connecting operations to a materiality, instead of imposing a form upon a matter. [211]

It is that singularities, as Deleuze and Guattari clearly denote, always already reside within matter, as the energetic points, which contribute to its taking form or becoming. This becoming as I have discussed, emerges out as the process of those interconnected multiplicities that form the plane of immanence. I will proceed to explicate the Deleuzean multiplicities, and eventually singularities, with the help of a mathematical reading of both, since Deleuze and Guattari's description delineates a certain topological nature of singularity, as opposed to a geometrical one.

For the purpose of first clarifying multiplicities, I resort to the differential geometry of Riemann, who applies the term *mannigfaltigkeit* or manifold in order to assert a new approach to the mathematical thinking of space. The Riemannian multiplicity suggests an amalgamation of local spaces and the multiple transformations, or passages, between them. Riemann's aim is first and foremost to formulate a conception of space, more precisely; the aim is to consider space as the ontological ground, as opposed to Cantor's set theory, where space is designated by a particular set of points. The reason why Riemannian differential geometry is pertinent lies in its refusal of some pre-given set or assemblies of points from which determinate spatial relations occur. In simple words, Riemannian continuous manifolds or multiplicities is an immanent process, whereas set theory is closer to the transcendental which is, of course, frowned upon in Deleuzean philosophy. In practical mathematical terms, the Riemannian continuous manifolds enable a two-dimensional surface to be investigated without embedding it in a frame of reference, or a three-dimensional space.

Riemann's manifold is an extension of Gauss's approach, regarding the internal geometry of curved surfaces. This idea frees geometry from the ambient three-dimensional Euclidean space against which they are set and referenced and, as such, it is not a question of curvatures in flat space, but what Riemann affirms is that the space itself is curved.

Additionally, the structure of space and its curvature vary from point to point; in any given event all spaces are investigated according to their own terms, independent of any pre-given ambient or primary space of reference.

So far, all I have been describing corresponds in philosophical terms to the Deleuzean plane of immanence, that topological space of amalgamated multiplicities. Moreover, the Riemannian consideration of the space itself as being curved proposes that the space or precisely the curvature is made up of infinitesimal points, which allow for a variable number of dimensions for the space to be studied on its own.

The manifold is highly useful as it simplifies investigating dynamic behavior, especially when applied to physical systems for instance. Accordingly, the manifold, or the curvature of space, corresponds to the possible states of the physical system, and alternately its dimensions represent the changes in the states of the system enabling the location of those specific points along the curve where change occurs.

This simplification brings forth new topological attributes such as points where the curvature takes an infinite value. This attractor point determines the behavior of the curvature itself, and relatively of the system as a whole. Jules-Henri Poincaré refers to these points as singularities. They are specifically these attractors[212], which lead the distribution of the infinitesimal points that make up the curve and as a result govern its behavior. For Deleuze, singularities are "points of departure for a series which extends over all the ordinary points of the system, as far as the region of another singularity which gives rise to another series which may either converge or diverge from the first." [213]

Nevertheless, singularities are not to be confused with, or considered as, the target towards which matter tends, but they are exactly what the actualization of matter, through differentiation, is attracted towards. In going back to mathematics, differential geometry in particular, let me illustrate the importance of topology in contrast to Euclidean geometry. I take the example of a triangle and a quadrilateral. Under Euclidean geometry, they are two completely different geometric figures, however in topology they are both equivalent to one another.

A triangle topologically is transformed into a quadrilateral by simply folding one of its vertices. Under topology, geometric figures are deformed or transformed. The triangle, in this case, transforms into a quadrilateral by folding over one of its vertices, alternately the quadrilateral is deformed into a triangle via another process of folding. Furthermore, both the triangle and the quadrilateral can become other geometric figures, which gets me to the pertinence of singularities. As we now know, singularities define, or govern, the orientation of the series of infinitesimal points as attractors towards which the curvature tends.

Singularities never appear in a topological space, although they positively produce or actualize each figure. What appears or emanates in topology are the ordinary points of geometrical figures, i.e. the vertices.

In this regard, singularities are never given, they do not take on any form, they are what makes up the differential fabric, so to speak, of topological space, they are present as their presence is inferred from the transformation of figures. "Attractors are never actualized, since no point of a trajectory ever reaches the attractor itself." [214]

Singularities present the conditions for actualization, for the becoming of geometrical figures, in this case, without being found in the final form or without themselves being actualized.

In simple Deleuzean words, topological space corresponds to the virtual plane, a continuum of singularities:

> Figures which are completely distinct in Euclidean geometry (a triangle, a square, or a circle, for example) become one and the same figure, since they can be deformed into one another. In this sense,

> topology may be said to be the least differentiated geometry, the one with the least number of distinct equivalence classes, the one in which many discontinuous forces have blended into one continues one. [215]

Additionally, singularities play another role in the actualization process, as attractors to the points of curvature; they identify the threshold at which differentiated figures emerge, in order to generate radically new geometric figures. The threshold is that point where we move from one topological space into the next, where the becoming figure is open to infinite possibilities.

Borges, in the *Aleph,* alludes on the singularity without mentioning it. Around the end, after his ineffable experience, having been intoxicated by it, he cannot find the words nor the linguistic structure to describe it. He mentions how language is successive, hence it is rather difficult to put down in words what his eyes concurrently saw. However, Borges is no novice when it comes to wording, and he elaborately writes, apropos of singularity that is:

> Each thing (a mirror's face, let us say) was infinite things, since I distinctly saw it from every angle of the universe. I saw the teeming sea; I saw daybreak and nightfall; I saw the multitudes of America; I saw a silvery cobweb in the center of a black pyramid; I saw a splintered labyrinth (it was London); I saw, close up, unending eyes watching themselves in me as in a mirror; I saw all the mirrors on earth and none of them reflected me; I saw in a backyard of Soler Street the same tiles that thirty years before I'd seen in the entrance of a house in Fray Bentos; I saw bunches of grapes, snow, tobacco, lodes of metal, steam; I saw convex equatorial deserts and each one of their grains of sand; I saw a woman in Inverness whom I shall never forget; I saw her tangled hair, her tall figure, I saw the cancer in her breast.[216]

Not only do we find in Borges's words that which describes the singularity, and complements the mathematical explanation of it, but an insight, a pragmatic approach to the very changing nature of singularities.

Singularities themselves change and mutate, as a corollary of the events they instigate, some appear others disappear; this characteristic is at the heart of the virtual.

Singularities and the Idea: Differential Geometry and Deleuze

The divergence of singularities, their change, as well as their very governance as attractors, is affirmed by the Idea, as "they establish a kind of resonance between divergent series."[217]

So far, as Deleuze has remarked, Ideas are not actual, rather purely virtual. Ideas are formed by the virtual multiplicities, whence all differential relations and singularities, which govern and lead the process of individuation, coexist:

> In the first place, Ideas are incarnated in fields of individuation: the intensive series of individuating factors envelop ideal singularities which are in themselves pre-individual; the resonances between series put the ideal relations in play.
>
> Second, Ideas are actualized in species and parts, qualities and extensities, which cover and develop these fields of individuation. A species is made up of differential relations between genes, just as the organic parts and the extensity of a body are made up of actualized pre-individual singularities. However, the absolute condition of non-resemblance must be emphasized: neither species nor qualities resemble the differential relations that they actualize, any more than the organic parts resemble the singularities.[218]

On page 165 of *Difference and Repetition*, in elucidating the relationship of singularites to the Idea, Deleuze provides an example congruent with Leibniz's referral to the Idea of the sea, as designating a system of differential relations and singularities:

> Leibniz has a metaphor that he likes: you are near the sea and you listen to waves. You listen to the sea and you hear the sound of a wave. I hear the sound of a wave, that is, I have an apperception: I distinguish a wave. And Leibniz says: you would not hear the wave if you did not have a minute unconscious perception of the sound of each drop of water that slides over and through another, and that makes up the object of minute perceptions. There is the roaring of all the drops of water, and you have your little zone of clarity, you clearly and distinctly grasp one partial result from this infinity of drops, from this infinity of roaring, and from it, you make your own little world, your own property.[219]

Every individual aspect possesses its own perspective which emerges out of the conglomeration of singularities, meshed into the differential field. In terms of perception, Deleuze as well as Leibniz suggest that conscious perception, our ability to discern the movement of the waves in this case, stems out from the differentiation of unconscious perceptions, the sound of the waves, or to be precise the sound of the aggregates of every drop of water forming the waves. We grasp a partial result or an actualization from the infinite permutations the drops may undergo in their virtual field through a process of differentiation lead by singularities. My perception of the Idea of the sea is accounted for by the actualization of the drops of water forming the waves of the sea, as an auditory sensation.

Moreover, learning to swim entitles a conjunction of the singularities of our bodies with those of the Idea of the sea; this is what forms a problematic field. Learning for Deleuze is an act of submergence into the system of differential relations that forms the universal problematic of the Idea and its corresponding singularities. In Leibniz's example, the sea is such a problematic Idea, namely that of the differential relation between the interaction of its dynamic water particles and the singularities guiding those particles towards the potentiality of functioning as waves.

"To learn is to enter into the universal of the relation which constitute the Idea, and into their corresponding singularities."[220] In other words, waves are an actualization (physical) of the water particles by way of a distinctive set of singularities in the midst of the sea (pun intended) of differential relations.

Deleuze goes a step further to elaborate on the relationship between the body of the swimmer as a concrete actual and the sea, in turn another body or actual domain. When the swimmer is immersed in the sea, the singularities, which are embodied in the swimmer, conjoin with those embodied in the sea, and form the virtual problematic field, and "it is this conjugation of singularities that determines for us a threshold of consciousness at which our real acts are adjusted to our perceptions of the real relations thereby providing a solution to the problem."[221]

The same approach applies to Young's experiment, most widely known as the double slit experiment. Singularities embedded in the slits conjoin with the singularities of light thus forming the virtual field of the problematic Idea, and by way of this conjunction, the threshold of consciousness is determined, how the physicist adjusts what he perceives as the end result on the screen, and thereby provides a positing to the problem of the nature of light: the wave-particle duality.

However, Deleuze is swift to resolve the incapacity and limitations of a *strictly* conscious led active perception, as perception that posits the universal problematic. His resolution comes by way of signs. But before I elaborate on the notion of sign, or actually recollect what I have already written on Deleuzean signs, let me display the shortcomings of consciousness *alone* in this context.

The modus operandi of consciousness resorts to common sense and memory; it is through the relationship of knowledge from past experiences, and the Symbolic order, that I am able to perceive something, even if it is the first time I do so, I make sense of it with what I already know. In doing so, especially in the case of the problematic field of differentiated relations and its conglomerate singularities, or in my perception of the problematic Idea as such, I risk relegating this perception to semblance, or analogy, with what is already pre-given, or worse the reduction of the problematic idea itself to one of its preexisting historical solutions. Therefore I am unable to think pure difference, or grasp the emergence of the truly new.

Deleuze asserts "problems and their symbolic fields stand in relationship with signs,"[222] or as I have previously mentioned, solutions are signs to problems, "to learn is indeed to constitute this space of an encounter with signs." [223]

Buoyancy, keeping warm by moving, breathing slower and deeper, and relaxing muscles, all are answers, signs which indicate the problem that emerges from the conjugation of the singularities immanent in both human body and sea.

Once the swimmer perceives or is conscious of those signs and eventually passes the threshold of consciousness, his real live actions start to follow, or "are adjusted to his perceptions of the real relations of the sea."[224]

In Andrei Tarkovsky's *Stalker* from 1979, the protagonist works as a guide leading people through a supernatural Zone, where all the normal laws of physics seem suspended, towards a room which is said to grant the wishes of anyone who stands within its space. Against his wife's incessant pleas not to enter the Zone, the Stalker meets with two clients, a writer and a professor, wishing to visit the room. They need him to navigate the rough and unwelcoming terrain of the Zone, which he is very well familiar with. All three make their way towards the room led by the Stalker himself, who utilizes an apparatus made of metal knots and cloth to test for invisible traps.

Along the way, each of the two discloses his personal reasons for seeking the room; the writer is desperate as he is losing his inspiration, and therefore his ability to write, or to pen down with the aid of language, experiences and thoughts he has been having, which have been becoming more frustrating recently. As for the professor, he only seeks the room to win a Nobel prize.

Stalker, in turn, divulges that he is not the first to navigate the Zone and guide clients in. There was a predecessor, Porcupine, from whom he has learnt and acquired everything there is to know about the Zone, and respectively the room. Porcupine accompanied his brother into the room leading him to his demise. Then Porcupine went back afterwards, a visit which rendered him wealthy, but soon enough he committed suicide. They stop at the entrance to the room, where the writer and the professor change their mind, and decide not to enter anymore. The writer suggests Porcupine's misfortune is due to the nature of the room, its mechanism so to speak: despite Porcupine's conscious wish to resuscitate his brother, the room granted him his unconscious desire for wealth, so unable to live with himself, he committed suicide. Then it starts to rain, and the rain enters the room from a hole in the ceiling, rather befitting Gordon Matta-Clark's work. All three return to the bar whence there journey has started. The Stalker returns home to his wife and child, and in a conversation admits to his wife that those who call themselves writers and scientists do not believe in anything, as if "they have the organ with which one believes atrophied for lack of use…they have empty eyes." [225]

Schirmacher suggests that *Geviert* does not arise solely from architecture and urban planning, but those should be supplemented with film and media as well. Tarkovsky's *Stalker* provides this unifying supplement, in order to bring together all three approaches to the fourfold thinking and praxis. First of all, I start with the main character in the film, the Stalker, to whom I assign the characteristics of a romantic revolutionary. He seeks the satisfaction and liberation of others, the accomplishment of wishes, an idealized state where everyone has what they need and want, a selfless figure ready to sacrifice all for his cause. He is of course a repetition of a previous stalker, one that has failed in safeguarding his brother, and eventually strayed from his proper revolutionary ideals to be governed by his unconscious desires for power and wealth, and in his regret ended his life; here one is tempted to think of failed historical revolutions.

What causes the Stalker to fall into despair, at the very end of the film, is the lack of belief exhibited by his clients. In a previous comment, where the writer speculates about the nature of the room and its process, he suggests that it is useless for those with resoluteness, yet dangerous for those who desire it.

Those who attempt it in desire are hindered—shortsighted by their need to satisfy—act upon that which they desire. Let me consider the room in terms of the topological Riemannian space, and consequently the Deleuzean problematic of the Idea; what is missing in the room is the threshold of consciousness itself. The subjects lacking such a threshold are unable to read the granted wishes or answers as signs of the problem, and thus are lacking the problematic Idea itself. Porcupine killed himself when he came to such a conclusion, when he realized that his wealth is a sign of the problem that he truly did not care about his brother, but more about his own selfish desires. This much of the writer's speculations are true. On the contrary, it is not that those already equipped with resoluteness do not receive anything from the room, or that the room does not give them an answer, but they are the ones who see everything, who look into the *Aleph*, and experience Matta-Clark's liberated spaces as calm, selfless, and embracing the universal. The Stalker in the film is an enabler of the *Aleph*. He could be understood as someone who clears space for the fourfold, whereas his clients with empty eyes cannot see what he sees, for they lack. Interestingly enough, among the characters in the film, apart from the Stalker himself, it is his wife who believes, even if she had never been through the Zone and into the room, even when she has not perceived. But it is precisely this seeing that is characteristic of the fourfold. In his moment of despair, where he confesses to her that no one needs the room, she assures him and tells him he should not be angry but pity them. When he says that no one believes and no one can see, she genuinely offers to accompany him there. Later on in a strange monologue addressed right into the camera, she confesses her love for him in spite of the many warnings against them being together and the hardship of their life together so far.

It is through the throwness of love that her eyes are filled; she sees, she believes, and in the proper Buddhist manner she is free. This is mentioned in the Stalker's dialogue as he says to her, when she offers to be led into the Zone and to the room, that she will get nothing from the room, it will not work for her. Moreover in her direct confessions, her affections for the Stalker seem to be along the following lines:

> "Let there be spaces in your togetherness, and let the winds of the heavens dance between you. Love one another but make not a bond of love: Let it rather be a moving sea between the shores of your souls."[226]

A moving sea, a bridge between the two banks, the site for the gathering of the fourfold, as Heidegger asserts.

It was Borges in the Aleph who upon seeing his dead lover's face became vertiginous and wept, "for my eyes had seen that secret and conjectured object whose name is common to all men but which no man has looked upon —the unimaginable universe."[227] And it is only through authentic love that such universality presents itself, and it does so not "as a regularization of the particular, but as a singularity,"[228] and it is in this precise sense that one should understand revolution.

8. Conclusion: Deactualization as the Authentic Revolutionary Praxis

Deleuze and Guattari's Deterritorialization

The term deterritorialization appears throughout the collaborative works of Gilles Deleuze and Felix Guattari, and in its many contexts comes to signify varying notions, or more accurately its use is thought specific. For my interest, I borrow deterritorialization from *A Thousand Plateaus: Capitalism and Schizophrenia*, where the authors interpret it as a spatial notion that produces change. In their use in this context, Deleuze and Guattari assign to deterritorialization, the traits of singularities, or attractors, in such a manner that deterritorialization designates what is inherent to an area of space and which "directs" that area towards immanent change.

Moreover, recall the example of the triangle and the quadrilateral, which if studied in a topological space are both equivalent within the same space, but given more than one topological space by way of the threshold, and the geometric figure is transformed infinitely by a multiplicity of differential relations. As a result, one might say the notion of deterritorialization designates the coupling of singularities and thresholds, or to borrow from mathematical vocabulary, it is a vector. With both direction and magnitude, deterritorialization is that which differentiates any spatial area as it repeats it—of course by now the term repetition strictly corresponds to change.

Relatively, deterritorialization asserts the experience of creative difference, and thus the emergence of pure becoming. The splitting praxis of Matta-Clark is an example of such deterritorialization. There is no longer an originary point, that fixed point which determines and consequently pre-conditions all other points in space to converge towards its sameness, that is the building is 'freed' from the rigidity of historical architectural structuring, but there exists a liberated space, a spacing which generates infinitesimal and infinite points each with its own coordinates, independent of any system or space of reference. Instead of "here" and "there", there is the space which gathers "here", "there", and in-between in an eternally open site (the universal), and through this process, everything is immanently differentiated and the radically new can emerge. Succinctly put, deterritorialization is the process by which what was actual is de-actualized so to speak, and reconstituted back into the virtual domain where it is apt for possibility of its different re-actualization.

Moreover, in considering the psychoanalytic aspect of deterriotirialization, I will first resort to the Lacanian concept of territorialization. For Lacan, at the earliest stages, the infant, still unable to differentiate between itself and the Other, experiences an excess of pleasure in the domain of the Real. There is nothing for the infant but its needs which are fully satisfied, or as Lacan denotes it, an experience of completeness. However, as soon as the infant starts recognizing itseself and experiencing its body through the mother's attentiveness to its erogenous zones: mouth, anus, penis or vagina, and its correspondence to the infant's development of its libidinal attachments, and to partial objects, it sustains "territorialization." Additionally, the entrance of the infant into the Symbolic order enhances this process of territorialization, as its needs undergo symbolization and signification through language, which further evade their satisfaction.

What deterritorialization does, in this case, is liberate the organs and in turn the subject from identifying with the fulfillment of the lack.

There is a term in Tibetan Buddhism known as *Dzogchen*. It is said to be the state of clarity and pure openness, a state that perceives, experiences, and expresses and informs everything. Moreover, this state is immanent and is never affected by what it informs nor by the actualities it brings forth. For Buddhists, *Dzogchen*'s relation with reality is analogous to that of a mirror and its reflection; whatever is reflected is of no effect on the mirror.[229] For a Buddhist to step out of the circle of suffering, to break free from Saṃsāra, they have to be liberated from desiring that which stands in for the lack, and to do so is to stop identifying objects with the possibility of the fulfillment of the lacking satisfaction. In this regard, Buddhism can be considered to be a process of deterritorialization; one that de-actualizes the order of the Symbolic, of language, symbolizations, representations, and semblance, back into the plane of immanence of Ideas or the *Dzogchen* which is at the very heart of the Idea.

In her direct monologue, the Stalker's wife confesses to what she calls "bitter happiness", where she had to sacrifice all worldly delights and pleasures, the "wealthy life", in the name of her love for her husband, and in doing so she acknowledges her sacrifice as being a sign for the problematic of Idea, love in this case. She could only grasp the Idea by way of such a deterritorialization, only by renouncing to pursue materialistic possessions and selfish interests, that she is able to love the Stalker in the way she does, and she does confess so to herself and to the audience in that threshold moment of consciousness where she could grasp the "moving sea" of love. It is only through this process of moving back into the virtual field that one is able to think/grasp the Idea. In other words, it is by way of supplementing the field of the Idea, with its de-actualized signs, by process of deterritorialization, and therefore reestablishing the differential relations, adding to that the conjugation between the singularities immanent in all these de-actualized multiplicities. All of this leads to the production of universality:

> On the one hand, in the progressive determination of the conditions, we must in effect discover the adjunctions which complete the initial field of the problem as such - in other words, the varieties of the multiplicity in all its dimensions, the fragments of ideal future or past events which, by the same token, render the problem solvable; and we must establish the modality in which these enclose or are connected with the initial field. On the other hand, we must condense all the singularities, precipitate all the circumstances, points of fusion, congelation or condensation in a sublime occasion, *Kairos*, which makes the solution explode like something abrupt, brutal and revolutionary.[230]

This explosion of the universal happens at the propitious moment, where at his weakest[231], the wife stays by the Stalker's side, comforting him and declaring her love for him, that proper threshold moment.

Moment of Clarity: Schirmacher, Media, and Multiperspectivity

In *Media as LifeWorld*, Wolfgang Schirmacher attests to the fact that leaving the comfort of the definite, the pre-given, and determined—that which is representative—in favor of a multiplicities and infinite possibilities of interpretation is generally resisted:

> Yet although the distinctions between reality and imagination, truth and fantasy seem to vanish, and the acceptance of media as an authentic lifeworld the next step, media theory is still reluctant to face this consequence. Signification, representation, and the ideology of an independent reality as the measure of truth - these are compelling and long-held presuppositions not easily cast aside.[232]

As a corollary to such a fastening, perception is relegated to a confined space governed by a central fixed point, in relation to which everything is signified and represented.

Moreover, Schirmacher notes that the security of the definite and pre-given is inherent to the sense of (personal) space. He suggests however, that such resistance to do away with the old familiar and definite is combated by media itself, as the case of music videos reveals the absence of personal space. Ruptured and decentralized, it gives way to temporality which "has become ever more important, incorporating all that which has formerly the realm of spatiality."[233] From media, Schirmacher is able to extract several approaches or practices that prove viable in the production of "multiperspectivity". "The layering [of images] create, by superimposition of different perspectives, hyperreality which is according to Merleau-Ponty more real than reality."[234]

Creative Rethinking

As I have shown, it is reality, as semblance, that hinders the "discovery of the real as pure surface," and it is only through hyperreality as deterritorializing reality that we are exposed to the Real. Maybe it is through media that one might perceive the problematic of the Idea.[235]

And in this sense, what is lacking in today's revolutionaries is this "multiperspectivity", the ability to "superimpose" the multiplicities which make up the virtual field, and to leave that *between*, for this is the plane where singularities condense and differentiation occurs, and multiplicities open up unto the infinite possibilities to become.

Recent revolutionary attempts are far from the Idea, as action driven, they are caught in the turning of the wheel of time; a cyclical failed repetition led by semblance and passed on historical structures. They are the pursuit of accomplishing that which is potentiality, what will be, the expected fixed point in the future, and this is precisely what should be resisted: aiming towards a definitive goal, establishing a set of demands and marching on in the name of a cause. It is only when there are no demands, no proposed solutions, and no definitive future potentiality to be realized, that true multiperspectivity exists—calmness unto the *Geviert or Dzogchen*—the problematic presents itself as the universality of the Idea, and in that atemporal moment of vision, "time forks perpetually toward innumerable futures." [236]

In the end I repeat, it is time to take a step back, think and then do the right thing. What we need is the moment of clarity, since it is only then that we have a chance for rethinking the Idea of revolution as such; the *public use of reason*, of suspending action, of thinking and as Žižek puts it, "without this moment of authentic passivity nothing New can emerge."[237]

Endnotes

[1] Wolfgang Schirmacher, "Technoculture and Life Technique" in *Just Living: Philosophy in Artificial Life*. New York: Atropos, n.d. N. pag. *European Graduate School*. Web. 01 Oct. 2013. http://www.egs.edu/faculty/wolfgang-schirmacher/articles/technoculture-and-life-technique/

[2] Wolfgang Schirmacher, *ibid.*

[3] Wolfgang Schirmacher, *Homo Generator in the Postmodern Discussion. From a Conversation with Jean-François Lyotard.* European Graduate School. N.p., n.d. Web. 01 Oct. 2013. http://www.egs.edu/faculty/wolfgang-schirmacher/articles/homo-generator-in-the-postmodern-discussion/

[4] Jean Baudrillard , *Contemporary Art: Art Contemporary with Itself.* Trans. Chris Turner. *The Intelligence of Evil or the Lucidity Pact (Talking Images)*. N.p.: Berg, 2005. N. pag. *European Graduate School*. Web. 01 Sept. 2012. http://www.egs.edu/faculty/jean-baudrillard/articles/contemporary-art-art-contemporary-with-itself/

[5] John, Rajchman, *Constructions* (Cambridge, MA: MIT, 1998), 8.

[6] See Alain Badiou " The Idea of Communism".

[7] Franco Berardi, *The Uprising: On Poetry and Finance* (Los Angeles: Semiotext(e), 2012) 7.

[8] Franco Berardi *ibid.*, 8.

[9] Franco Berardi *ibid.*,9.

[10] Slavoj Žižek, "The Communist Hypothesis" in *First as Tragedy, Then as Farce* (London: Verso, 2009), 87.

[11] Michael Hardt and Antonio Negri, *Take Up the Baton,* Jacobin A Magazine of Culture and Polemics. N.p., n.d. Web. 04 Oct. 2013. https://www.jacobinmag.com/2012/05/take-up-the-baton/

[12] Bruno Latour, *Some Experiments in Art and Politics,* E-flux. N.p., n.d. Web. 4 Sept. 2013. http://www.e-flux.com/journal/some-experiments-in-art-and-politics/

[13] Bruno Latour *ibid.*

[14] Bruno Latour *ibid.*

[15] Perhaps people hate being in between things, they simply do not know what to do in that case, and this always translates into them acting, even if it were a rash decision.

[16] See Douglas Adams, *The Hitchhiker's Guide to the Galaxy* (New York: Harmony, 1980).

[17] Slavoj Žižek, "Occupy Wall Street: What Is to Be Done Next?" *Theguardian.com*. Guardian News and Media, 24 Apr. 2012. Web. 24 Apr. 2012. http://www.theguardian.com/commentisfree/cifamerica/2012/apr/24/occupy-wall-street-what-is-to-be-done-next

[18] Wolfgang Schirmacher "On the Inability to Recognize the Human Flaw" in *Just Living: Philosophy in Artificial Life*. New York: Atropos, n.d. N. pag. *European Graduate School*. Web. 30 Aug. 2013. http://www.egs.edu/faculty/wolfgang-schirmacher/articles/on-the-inability-to-recognize-the-human-flaw/

[19] Alain Badiou, *Deleuze: The Clamor of Being* (Minneapolis: U of Minnesota, 2000) 112.

[20] Jean Baudrillard, "Contemporary Art: Art Contemporary with Itself." Trans. Chris Turner. *The Intelligence of Evil or the Lucidity Pact (Talking Images)*. N.p.: Berg, 2005. N. pag. *European Graduate School*. Web. 01 Sept. 2012. http://www.egs.edu/faculty/jean-baudrillard/articles/contemporary-art-art-contemporary-with-itself/

[1] See Daniel Bensaïd, *Marx for Our Times: Adventures and Misadventures of a Critique* (London: Verso, 2002).

\[22] If one were to look up the word revolution in a dictionary those are the definitions found.

[23] Hans Siegbert. Reiss, "The Conflict of Faculties" in *Kant: Political Writings* (Cambridge: Cambridge UP, 1991) 182.

[24] See Jerry Rubin, *Do It; Scenarios of the Revolution* (New York: Simon and Schuster, 1970).

[25] The term "Spring" is an allusion to the French Revolution of 1848, referred to as the Springtime of the People, and to the waves of protests in Prague in 1968.

[26] On April 1st 2014 thousands of gathered in front of the supreme electoral council in Ankara to call for a recount of the electoral result. The crowd proceeded to clash with the riot police who used teargas and water cannons to disperse the protestors.

[27] Slavoj Žižek, "Occupy Wall Street: What Is to Be Done Next?" *Theguardian.com*. Guardian News and Media, 24 Apr. 2012. Web. 24 Apr. 2012. http://www.theguardian.com/commentisfree/cifamerica/2012/apr/24/occupy-wall-street-what-is-to-be-done-next

[28] Slavoj Žižek *ibid.*

[29] See Martin Heidegger, *What Is Called Thinking?* Trans. Fred D. Wieck (New York: Harper & Row, 1968).

[30] Immanuel Kant, and Mary J. Gregor, "What Is Enlightenment?" in *Practical Philosophy* (Cambridge: Cambridge UP, 1996), 18.

[31] Immanuel Kant, *ibid.*

[32] T. J. Clark, "Painting in the Year Two", in Representations, No. 47, Special Issue: National Cultures before Nationalism (Summer, 1994) 13–63.

[33] Incidentally this recreation features on the cover of the DVD version of the documentary. Moreover the documentary deals with the transformative power of art. Muniz said the recreation of David's painting was accidental. While at the landfill, he spotted two pickers carrying a bathtub, which made him think of Marat.

[34] Walter Benjamin, *The Arcades Project* (Cambridge, MA: Belknap, 1999) 482.

[35] In this precise sense, there is a scene from the Matrix, where Morpheus shows Neo images of the waste land, as he says "This is the real world", Only a "future developer" like Morpheus could show Neo that there is nothing but waste.

[36] Slavoj Žižek, *The Pervert's Guide To Ideology*, Dir. Sophie Fiennes (Zeitgeist Films, 2012).

[37] Gilles Deleuze, "Asymmetrical Synthesis of the Sensible" in *Difference and Repetition* (New York: Columbia UP, 1994) 222.

[38] Slavoj Žižek, "The Pure Difference" in *Less than Nothing: Hegel and the Shadow of Dialectical Materialism* (London: Verso, 2012) 608.

[39] Slavoj Žižek, *The Puppet and the Dwarf: The Perverse Core of Christianity* (Cambridge, MA: MIT, 2003) 94-95.

[40] Peter Hallward, *Out of This World: Deleuze and the Philosophy of Creation* (London: Verso, 2006) 15.

[41] Gilles Deleuze, "Difference in Itself" in *Difference and Repetition* (New York: Columbia UP, 1994) 59.

[42] Gilles Deleuze *Ibid.*, 183.

[43] Georg Wilhelm Friedrich Hegel, *The Philosophy of History* (New York: Dover Publications, 1956) 313.

[44] Slavoj Žižek, "Ergo: the Dialectical Nonsequitur" in *Tarrying with the Negative* (Durham: Duke UP, 1993) 150.

[44] See Slavoj Žižek, *In Defense of Lost Causes* (London: Verso, 2008).

[45] Slavoj Žižek, "The Thing in Itself: Hegel" in *Less than Nothing: Hegel and the Shadow of Dialectical Materialism* (London: Verso, 2012), 290.

[46] Heine, Heinrich, and Charles Godfrey Leland. "French Affairs: The

Citizen Kingdom" in *The Works of Heinrich Heine*. Vol. 14 (London: W. Heinemann, 1891).

[47] Slavoj Žižek, "The Limits of Hegel" in *Less than Nothing: Hegel and the Shadow of Dialectical Materialism* (London: Verso, 2012) 481.

[48] See Gilles Deleuze, *Difference and Repetition* (New York: Columbia UP, 1994).

49 See Paradise of Bachelors Catalogue.

[50] Slavoj Žižek, "The Political Suspension of the Ethical" in *Less than Nothing: Hegel and the Shadow of Dialectical Materialism* (London: Verso, 2012) 998.

[51] See Karl Marx, Eden Paul, and Cedar Paul, *The Eighteenth Brumaire of Louis Bonaparte* (London: G. Allen & Unwin, 1926).

[52] Where is this?

[53] Karl Marx, *ibid.*

[54] Gilles Deleuze, *Difference and Repetition* (New York: Columbia UP, 1994) 10.

[55] Gilles Deleuze, *Difference and Repetition* (New York: Columbia UP, 1994) 268.

[56] See Marx Brothers *Night at the Opera*. Dir. George S. Kaufman, Chico Marx, Groucho Marx, Harpo Marx, and Sam Wood.

[57] Marx Brothers, *ibid.*

[58] This third moment is by no means the synthesis of the first two, but should be understood as a continuation of the Idea. Repetition persists, but always as difference.

[59] Gilles Deleuze, *Difference and Repetition* (New York: Columbia UP, 1994) 41.

[60] A May '68 posters showing de Gaulle holding a riot baton behind his back, as his other hand pats a representation of France. The Poster reads: "Votez toujours, je ferai le reste." Just vote, and keep the rest to me.

[61] See Jean Francois Lyotard *La Condition Postmoderne: Rapport sur le Savoir* (Les Editions de Minuit, 1979).

[62] Wolfgang Schirmacher "After the Last Judgment: Hegel as Philosopher of Artificial Life" in *Just Living: Philosophy in Artificial Life*. New York: Atropos, n.d. N. pag. *European Graduate School*. Web. 30 Aug. 2013. http://www.egs.edu/faculty/wolfgang-schirmacher/articles/after-the-last-judgment/

[63] Wolfgang Schirmacher, *ibid.*

[64] *Soyez réalistes, demandez l'impossible was* one of the slogans most graffitied around Paris.

[65] A slogan of May '68 was "I am Marxist of the Groucho Tendency". This holds true for the farcical aspect of the events, *i.e.* how things turned out to be. However the events failed to grasp and invigorate that third moment, the realization of difference. And perhaps it is in the farcical sense that Occupy Wall Street "repeats" Paris 1968.

66 Wolfgang Schirmacher "After the Last Judgment: Hegel as Philosopher of Artificial Life" in *Just Living: Philosophy in Artificial Life*. New York: Atropos, n.d. N. pag. *European Graduate School*. Web. 30 Aug. 2013. http://www.egs.edu/faculty/wolfgang-schirmacher/articles/after-the-last-judgment/

[67] See Chris Marker *Sixties.*

[68] Chris Marker *Ibid.*

[69] Wolfgang Schirmacher "Technoculture and Life Technique" in *Just Living: Philosophy in Artificial Life*. New York: Atropos, n.d. N. pag. *European Graduate School*. Web. 30 Aug. 2013. http://www.egs.edu/faculty/wolfgang-schirmacher/articles/on-the-inability-to-recognize-the-human-flaw/

[70] Martin Heidegger, *Being and Time* (New York: Harper, 1962) 437.

[71] Martin Heidegger, *ibid.*

[72] Martin Heidegger, *ibid.*

[73] Recall Kierkegaard's notion of repetition, especially in this "orientational" aspect, where he posits repetition and recollection as the same movement, except in opposite directions.

[74] Fidel Castro declares this in a speech given on January 1961, for the second anniversary of the triumph of the revolution.

[75] See Henri Bergson, *Elan Vital.*

[76] Constantin V. Boundas, *Deleuze and Philosophy* (Edinburgh: Edinburgh UP, 2006) 297.

[77] Gilles Deleuze, *Difference and Repetition* (New York: Columbia UP, 1994) 186.

[78] Gilles Deleuze, *The Logic of Sense* (New York: Columbia UP, 1990) 22.

[79] Adrian Parr, "Virtual/Virtuality" in *The Deleuze Dictionary* (Edinburgh: Edinburgh UP, 2005) 298.

[80] Badiou, Alain. "The Event in Deleuze." Trans. John Roffe. *Parrhesia* 2 (n.d.): n. pag. *European Graduate School*. Web. 13 December 2012. http://www.egs.edu/faculty/alain-badiou/articles/the-event-in-deleuze/

[81] Alain Badiou, *ibid.*

[82] Alain Badiou, *ibid.*

[83] Alain Badiou, *ibid.*

[84] Alain Badiou *ibid.*

[85] Alain Badiou first alludes to what he calls "terme évanouissant" in *Theory of the Subject.*

[86] Alain Badiou "The Event in Deleuze" Trans. John Roffe. *Parhessia* 2 (n.d.): n. pag. *European Graduate School*. Web. 01 June 2014. http://www.egs.edu/faculty/alain-badiou/articles/the-event-in-deleuze/

[87] "The Higgs Boson Explained." PBS, n.d. Web. 02 Aug. 2012. www.pbs.org/wgbh/nova/blogs/physics/2012/06/the-higgs-boson-explained.

[88] Although it cannot be predicted whether any given atom of a radioactive substance will decay at any given time, the decay products of a radioactive substance are extremely predictable. Because of this, decay products are important to scientists in many fields who need to know the quantity or type of the parent product.

[89] Gilles Deleuze, *Difference and Repetition* (New York: Columbia UP, 1994) 154.

[90] See Michael Inwood, "Projection and the A Priori" in *A Heidegger Dictionary* (Malden, MA: Blackwell, 2000).

[91] Slavoj Žižek, "Deleuze's Platonism: Ideas as Real." *Lacan dot com.* N.p., n.d. Web. 12 Dec. 2013. http://www.lacan.com/zizplato.htm

[92] Slavoj Žižek, *ibid.*

[93] See David Spriggs.com

[94] David Spriggs, *ibid.*

[95] DavidSpriggs.com

[96] Wolfgang Schirmacher, "The Virtual Human - A Trans Without Qualities" in *Anthropologie Der Medien - Mensch Und Kommunikationstechnologien.* N.p.: n.p., 2002. N. pag. *European Graduate School*. Web. 20 Feb. 2014. http://www.egs.edu/faculty/wolfgang-schirmacher/articles/the-virtual-human/

[97] Gilles Deleuze, *Difference and Repetition* (New York: Columbia UP, 1994) 206.

[98] Gilles Deleuze *ibid.*, 207.

[99] Jacques Derrida, and Geoffrey Bennington, *The Beast and the Sovereign* (Chicago: U of Chicago, 2009) 180.

[100] Gilles Deleuze, *Difference and Repetition* (New York: Columbia UP, 1994) 208.

[101] Gilles Deleuze, *The Logic of Sense* (New York: Columbia UP, 1990) 118.

[102] Gilles Deleuze *ibid.*, 209.

[103] Gilles Deleuze, *Difference and Repetition* (New York: Columbia UP, 1994) 212.

[104] See Marcel Proust *Albertine Disparue.*

[105] James Williams, *Gilles Deleuze's Difference and Repetition: A Critical Introduction and Guide* (Edinburgh: Edinburgh UP, 2003) 27.

[106] See Michael Inwood, *A Heidegger Dictionary* (Malden, MA: Blackwell, 2000) 76.

[107] "First Thai Film to Compete for Golden Lion Premieres at Venice Film Festival." Interview. *International Herald Tribune*. N.p., 31 Aug. 2006. Web. www.iht.com

[108] See Alain Badiou and Nicolas Truong, *In Praise of Love* (New York: New, 2012).

[109] This is beautifully explained in Jonathan Demme's Silence of the Lambs. In a conversation between Dr. Hannibal Lecter and FBI agent Clarice Starling, to capture a serial killer on the loose, Dr. Lecter cleverly suggests to ask "of each particular thing: what is it in itself? What is its nature? What does he do, this man you seek?" to which Clarice answers "He kills women..."

Dr. Lecter replies "No. That is incidental. What is the first and principal thing he does? What needs does he serve by killing?"

Clarice: "Anger, um, social acceptance, and, huh, sexual frustrations, sir..."

Dr. Lecter: "No! He covets. That is his nature. And how do we begin to covet, Clarice? Do we seek out things to covet? Make an effort to answer now."

Clarice: "No. We just..."

Dr. Lecter: "No. We begin by coveting what we see every day. Don't you feel eyes moving over your body, Clarice? And don't your eyes seek out the things you want?"

[110] Alain Badiou and Nicolas Truong, *In Praise of Love* (New York: New, 2012) 22.

[111] James Williams, *Gilles Deleuze's Difference and Repetition: A Critical Introduction and Guide* (Edinburgh: Edinburgh UP, 2003) 200.

[112] Alain Badiou and Nicolas Truong, *In Praise of Love* (New York: New, 2012).

[113] Constantin V. Boundas, *Deleuze and Philosophy* (Edinburgh: Edinburgh UP, 2006) 297.

[114] Slavoj Žižek, "The Pure Difference" in *Less than Nothing: Hegel and the Shadow of Dialectical Materialism* (London: Verso, 2012) 608.

[115] Slavoj Žižek, *The Parallax View* (Cambridge, MA: MIT, 2006) 18.

116 Žižek refers to this gap as the hole in the Symbolic order. It is where the Real resists incorporation into the symbolic order, and thus remains a surplus and a compulsion.

[117] Alain Badiou and Nicolas Truong, *In Praise of Love* (New York: New, 2012) 65-66.

[118] Alain Badiou, "Eight Theses on the Universal" in *Lacan Dot Com* (n.d.): n. pag. *European Graduate School*. Web. 15 Mar. 2014. http://www.egs.edu/faculty/alain-badiou/articles/eight-theses-on-the-universal/

[119] Alain Badiou, *ibid.*

[120] Alain Badiou, *ibid.*

[121] Jacques Lacan mentioned this in a lecture once.

[122] The creation of the universe in a laboratory.

[123] Jonathan Lethem, *As She Climbed Across the Table* (Vintage Contemporaries, 1998) 13.

[124] Jonathan Lethem, *op. cit.*

[125] Jonathan Lethem, *ibid.,* 30.

[126] Jonathan Lethem, *ibid.,* 43.

[127] Jonathan Lethem, *ibid.,* 69.

[128] Had certain physical constants been slightly different, the universe would have been void of intelligent life.

[129] Jonathan Lethem, *As She Climbed Across the Table* (Vintage Contemporaries, 1998) 172.

[130] Alain Badiou, Wolfgang Schirmacher, and Slavoj Žižek, "On the Truth-Process" in *An Open Lecture* By Alain Badiou. European Graduate School, Saas-Fee. Aug. 2002. *European Graduate School*. Web. 12 June 2013. http://www.egs.edu/faculty/alain-badiou/articles/on-the-truth-process/

[131] Alain Badiou, "Eight Theses on the Universal" in *Lacan Dot Com* (n.d.): n. pag. *European Graduate School*. Web. 15 Mar. 2014. http://www.egs.edu/faculty/alain-badiou/articles/eight-theses-on-the-universal/

[132] Slavoj Žižek *Interrogating the Real,* edited by Rex Butler and Scott Stephens (London: Continuum, 2005, 2006) 195.

[133] Jonathan Lethem, *As She Climbed Across the Table* (Vintage Contemporaries, 1998) 58.

[134] Jonathan Lethem, *ibid.,* 57.

[135] Slavoj Žižek, "Reflections on WTC — Third Version" *Welcome to the Desert of the Real* (London: Verso, 2002). N. pag. *Lacan Dot Com*. Web. 28 June 2011. http://www.egs.edu/faculty/slavoj-zizek/articles/welcome-to-the-desert-of-the-real

[136] Slavoj Žižek, *ibid.*

[137] Alain Badiou *One Divides into Two* originally delivered in a series of lectures on April 1999 at the Collège International de Philosophie.

[138] Channel 4 HD aired the two episodes in 2012 in Great Britain.

[139] The Perseid meteor shower, one of the brighter meteor showers of the year, occur every August, peaking around August 9-13. Consisting of tiny space debris from the comet Swift-Tuttle, the Perseids are named after the constellation, Perseus. This is because, their *radiant* or the direction of which the shower seems to come from lies in the same direction as Perseus. The constellation lies in the north-eastern part of the sky.

[140] Daniel Smith, *Essays on Deleuze* (Edinburgh: Edinburgh UP, 2012) 22-23.

[141] Gilles Deleuze, *Difference and Repetition* (New York: Columbia UP, 1994) 63-64.

[142] This quote is attributed to Mahmoud Hojeij, where in his dissertation submitted to the Division of Media and Communications of the European Graduate School, he attests to Professor Schirmacher's proposed solution, that of making clear how problematic it is. See Mahmoud Hojeij *Becoming War: Failure, Penetration and Celebration* http://www.egs.edu/pdfs/mahmoud-hojeij-becoming-war.pdf

[143] Chris Drohan, *Toward a Material Concept of the Sign* (Diss. European Graduate School, 2006) 23. http://www.egs.edu/media/research-database/chris-drohan/

[144] Gilles Deleuze, *Proust and Signs* (New York: G. Braziller, 1972) 9.

[145] Slavoj Žižek, "Introduction to the Routledge Classic Edition" in *Organs Without Bodies: On Deleuze and Consequences*. (Abington, Oxon: Routledge, 2012).

[146] Alain Badiou *One Divides into Two* originally delivered in a series of lectures on April 1999 at the Collège International de Philosophie.

[147] Bruno Bosteels talks about drawing the consequences of a change, of a new situation, and if the change is evental then its consequences are infinite. See Bruno Bosteels, *Badiou and Politics*.

[148] Gilles Deleuze and Félix Guattari, *What Is Philosophy?* (New York: Columbia UP, 1994) 100.

[149] See Pete Wolfendale, Deleuze Some Common Misunderstandings in *Deontologistics* online weblog http://deontologistics.wordpress.

com/2009/08/04/deleuze-some-common-misunderstandings/

[150] Gilles Deleuze and Félix Guattari, *What Is Philosophy?* (New York: Columbia UP, 1994) 101.

[151] Alain Badiou, "The Event in Deleuze." Trans. John Roffe. *Parhessia* 2 (n.d.): n. pag. *European Graduate School*. Web. 13 December 2012. http://www.egs.edu/faculty/alain-badiou/articles/the-event-in-deleuze

[152] See Michael Inwood "Space and Spatiality" in *A Heidegger Dictionary* (Malden, MA: Blackwell, 2000).

[153] Gilles Deleuze in conversation with Antonio Negri From the journal *Futur Anterieur* 1(Spring 1990), translated by Martin Joughin.

[154] Gilles Deleuze, *Nietzsche and Philosophy* (New York: Columbia UP, 1983) 189.

[155] Gilles Deleuze, *Difference and Repetition* (New York: Columbia UP, 1994) 126.

[156] Gilles Deleuze, *Nietzsche and Philosophy* (New York: Columbia UP, 1983) 71.

[157] Catherine Malabou, "The Eternal Return and The Phantom of Difference" Trans. Arne De Boever. *Parrhesia* 10 (2010): 21-29. http://parrhesiajournal.org/parrhesia10/parrhesia10_malabou.pdf

[158] Catherine Malabou, *ibid.*

[159] Gilles Deleuze, *Nietzsche and Philosophy* (New York: Columbia UP, 1983) 46.

[160] Gilles Deleuze *ibid.*, 68.

[161] Michael Hardt, *Gilles Deleuze: An Apprenticeship in Philosophy* (Minneapolis: U of Minnesota, 1993) 18.

[162] Manuel DeLanda, *Deleuze and the Open-ended Becoming of the World.* Proc. of Chaos/Control: Complexity Conference, Universität Konstanz. 1998. Web. 14 Jan. 2014. http://www.egs.edu/faculty/manuel-de-landa/articles/deleuze-and-the-open-ended-becoming-of-the-world/

[163] Manuel DeLanda, *ibid.*

[164] Jacques Derrida and Maurizio Ferraris, *A Taste for the Secret* (Malden, MA: Polity, 2001) 20.

[165] See Slavoj Žižek's concluding chapter from *The Year of Dreaming Dangerously.*

[166] Martin Heidegger, "Building Dwelling Thinking." *Poetry, Language, Thought*. Trans. Albert Hofstadter. New York: Harper Colophon, 1971. N. pag. *Building Dwelling Thinking*. Web. 11 Mar. 2014. http://mysite.pratt.

edu/~arch543p/readings/Heidegger.html

[167] "Die Schwelle meint die Stelle des überschritts von einem Bezirk in den anderen." See Martin Heidegger *Gesamtausgabe* volume 52, p.37

[168] Arvo Pärt says "Tintinnabulation is like this. . . . The three notes of a triad are like bells. And that is why I call it tintinnabulation."

[169] See Albertcombrink.com

[170] Excerpt from the documentary *Arvo Pärt: 24 Preludes for a Fugue.*

[171] Gilles Deleuze, *Difference and Repetition* (New York: Columbia UP, 1994) 266.

[172] Arvo Pärt, Excerpt from the documentary *Arvo Pärt: 24 Preludes for a Fugue.*

[173] Arvo Pärt, *ibid.*

[174] Brian Morton and Pamela Collins, *Contemporary Composers* (Chicago: St. James, 1992) 729.

[175] Richard E. Rodda, liner notes for Arvo Pärt *Fratres, I Fiamminghi*, The Orchestra of Flanders, Rudolf Werthen, (Telarc CD-80387).

[176] See Samuel Beckett *Dieppe,* 1948.

[177] Georges Perec, *Species of Spaces and Other Pieces* (London, England: Penguin, 1997) 13.

[178] See Samuel Beckett *Dieppe,* 1948.

[179] Jacques Derrida, *The Post Card: From Socrates to Freud and beyond* (Chicago: U of Chicago, 1987) 121.

[180] Gordon Matta-Clark cited in Corinne Diseren (ed.), *Gordon Matta Clark*, (London & New York: Phaidon Press, 2003) 84.

[181] Martin Heidegger, "Building Dwelling Thinking" in *Poetry, Language, Thought.* Trans. Albert Hofstadter. New York: Harper Colophon, 1971. N. pag. *Building Dwelling Thinking.* Web. 11 Mar. 2014. http://mysite.pratt.edu/~arch543p/readings/Heidegger.html

[182] See Wolfgang Schirmacher *Media Philosophy and the Concept of Geviert* European Graduate School youtube channel. http://www.youtube.com/watch?v=SUNlXHm1ET0

[183] A rather precious advice by EGS Media and Communication Program Director Professor Wolfgang Schirmacher, where he proposes we talk about things as opposed to examining or being examined.

[184] Martin Heidegger, "Building Dwelling Thinking" in *Poetry, Language, Thought.* Trans. Albert Hofstadter. New York: Harper Colophon, 1971. N.

pag. *Building Dwelling Thinking*. Web. 11 Mar. 2014. http://mysite.pratt.edu/~arch543p/readings/Heidegger.html

[185] Jorge Luis Borges, *El Aleph*. Trans. Norman Thomas Di Giovanni (MIT Web) 6-7. http://web.mit.edu/allanmc/www/borgesaleph.pdf

[186] Jorge Luis Borges, *ibid.*, 8-9.

187 Gaston Bachelard, and M. Jolas, "Chapter 6" in *The Poetics of Space* (Boston: Beacon, 1994).

[188] Martin Heidegger, "Building Dwelling Thinking" in *Poetry, Language, Thought*. Trans. Albert Hofstadter. New York: Harper Colophon, 1971. N. pag. *Building Dwelling Thinking*. Web. 11 Mar. 2014. http://mysite.pratt.edu/~arch543p/readings/Heidegger.html

[189] Jorge Luis Borges, *El Aleph*. Trans. Norman Thomas Di Giovanni (MIT Web) 8. http://web.mit.edu/allanmc/www/borgesaleph.pdf

[190] Gordon Matta-Clark, Interview by François Vereesen. *Gordon Matta-Clark's Summer 77*. N.p., n.d. Web. 27 Apr. 2014. http://summer77.eu/applying-liberated-space

[191] Gordon Matta-Clark divulges this in an interview recorded by around the end of May 1977 in Diest, Belgium.

The interview was recorded after Matta-Clark's *the initial Office Baroque attempt* was refused by the city council. Matta-Clark is presented as an artist becoming an architect, a practice rather akin to Wolfgang Schirmacher's approach to the builder of the city as fourfold.

[192] Gordon Matta-Clark, *ibid.*

[193] Matta-Clark, *ibid.*

[194] Matta-Clark, *ibid.*

[195] Matta-Clark, *ibid.*

[196] The notion of nomadic time which I introduced and explained earlier, suggests the depravation of a fixed point of identity, and the differentiation of all the points which form a line of action of what Deleuze calls lines of flight. In Matta-Clark's case, the varying multiplicities of temporal moments present in his splitting, or opening up, spacing, of a given building, reveal each and every point as a point of differentiation, perceptively speaking. Moreover, it is through nomadic time that the camera allows for the ineffable experience to be shared.

[197] Matta-Clark, *ibid.*.

[198] Matta-Clark, *ibid.*

[199] Matta-Clark, *ibid.*

200 Wolfgang Schirmacher, "Die Stadt Als Geviert. Fragen Einer Philosophie Der Architektur." *European Graduate School*. N.p., n.d. Web. 17 Mar. 2014. www.egs.edu/faculty/wolfgang-schirmacher/articles/die-stadt-als-Geviert

[201] Slavoj Žižek, "The Tickling Object" in *The Parallax View* (Cambridge, MA: MIT, 2006) 17.

[202] Slavoj Žižek, "Architectural Parallax" in *Living at the End Times* (London: Verso, 2010) 245.

[203] Slavoj Žižek, *ibid.*

[204] See Adrian Parr, "Disjunctive Synthesis" in *The Deleuze Dictionary* (Edinburgh: Edinburgh UP, 2005) 97.

[205] J.G. Ballard, *High-Rise* (New York: Holt, Rinehart and Winston, 1977) 7.

[206] J.G. Ballard, *ibid.*

[207] Matta-Clark *op. cit.*

[208] J.G. Ballard, *High-rise* (New York: Holt, Rinehart and Winston, 1977) 204.

[209] Gilles Deleuze, *Difference and Repetition* (New York: Columbia UP, 1994) 176.

[210] Gilles Deleuze, *The Logic of Sense* (New York: Columbia UP, 1990) 36.

[211] Gilles Deleuze and Felix Guattari, "Treatise on Nomadology-The War Machine" in *A Thousands Plateaus* (London: Continuum, 1999) 408.

[212] Manuel DeLanda asserts in *Intensive Science and Virtual Philosophy* "singularities influence the behavior by acting as attractors for trajectories."

[213] Gilles Deleuze, *Difference and Repetition* (New York: Columbia UP, 1994) 278.

[214] Manuel DeLanda, *Intensive Science and Virtual Philosophy* (London: Continuum, 2002) 31-32.

[215] Manuel DeLanda, *ibid.*, 26

[216] Jorge Luis Borges, *El Aleph*. Trans. Norman Thomas Di Giovanni (MIT Web) 9. http://web.mit.edu/allanmc/www/borgesaleph.pdf

[217] Gilles Deleuze, *Difference and Repetition* (New York: Columbia UP, 1994) 278.

[218] Gilles Deleuze, *ibid.*, 279.

[219] Gilles Deleuze, "Deleuze/Leibniz." Cours Vincennes. Paris. 15 Apr. 1980. *Les Cours De Gilles Deleuze*. Web. 26 Apr. 2014. www.webdeleuze.com/php/texte.php?cle=50&groupe=Leibniz&langue=2

[220] Gilles Deleuze, *Difference and Repetition* (New York: Columbia UP, 1994) 165.

[221] Gilles Deleuze, *ibid.*

[222] Gilles Deleuze, *ibid.*,164.

[223] Gilles Deleuze, *ibid.*, 23.

[224] Gilles Deleuze, *ibid.*, 165.

[225] See Andrei Tarkovsky, *Stalker* (1979).

[226] See Khalil Gibran, "on Marriage" in *The Prophet* (Pan, 1991).

[227] Jorge Luis Borges, *op. cit.,* 9.

[228] Alain Badiou, "Eight Theses on the Universal" in *Lacan Dot Com* (n.d.): n. pag. *European Graduate School*. Web. 15 Mar. 2014. http://www.egs.edu/faculty/alain-badiou/articles/eight-theses-on-the-universal/

[229] As With Borges in the *Aleph.*

[230] Gilles Deleuze, *Difference and Repetition* (New York: Columbia UP, 1994) 190.

[231] The frailty of the Stalker can be considered analogous to the disappointed protesters, of our times, and it is only by encompassing such failure and disappointments that we are able to grasp the problematic of the Idea itself. This is what the wife does so perfectly well.

[232] Wolfgang Schirmacher, "Media as LifeWorld" in *Lifeworld and Technology*. Ed. Lester Embree. Washington, 1989. *European Graduate School.* Web. 17 Feb. 2014. www.egs.edu/faculty/wolfgang-schirmacher/articles/media-as-lifeworld/

[233] Wolfgang Schirmacher, *ibid.*

[234] Wolfgang Schirmacher, *ibid.*

[235] At the end of *Homo Generator: Media and the Postmodern Technology*, Professor Schirmacher attests to the fact that mediation is stripped from its original task of intervening between two conflicting parties, or sides, thus dismissing mediation as a dialectical process. Moreover, he suggests mediation is a creative process, that of media which enables us to cut, copy, rewind, superimpose, layer, zoom, composite, break, and so on. This frees mediation from anthropocentrism, and allows the bringing forth of the fourfold. http://www.egs.edu/faculty/wolfgang-schirmacher/articles/homo-generator-media-and-postmodern-technology/

[236] Jorge Luis Borges, *The Garden of Forking Paths* (1942). www.egs.edu/library/jorge-luis-borges/quotes/

[237] See Slavoj Žižek, *The Pervert's Guide To Ideology*, Dir. Sophie Fiennes (Zeitgeist Films, 2012).

Bibliography

Adams, Douglas. *The Hitchhiker's Guide to the Galaxy*. New York: Harmony, 1980.

Agamben, Giorgio, and William McCuaig. *Democracy in What State?* New York: Columbia UP, 2011.

Aristotle, and T. A. Sinclair. *The Politics*. Baltimore, MD: Penguin, 1962.

Arvo Pärt. *Alina*. Rec. July 1995. ECM New Series.

Badiou, Alain. *Being and Event*. London: Continuum, 2005.

---. *Deleuze: The Clamor of Being*. Minneapolis: U of Minnesota, 2000.

---. *Conditions*. London: Continuum, 2008.

---. "Eight Theses on the Universal." *Lacan Dot Com* (n.d.): n. pag. *European Graduate School*. Web. 15 Mar. 2014. <http://www.egs.edu/faculty/alain-badiou/articles/eight-theses-on- the-universal/>.

---. "The Event in Deleuze." Trans. John Roffe. *Parhessia* 2 (n.d.): n. pag. *European Graduate School*. Web. 01 June 2014. <http://www.egs.edu/faculty/alain-badiou/articles/the-event- in-deleuze/>.

Badiou, Alain, and Nicolas Truong. *In Praise of Love*. New York: New, 2012.

Bachelard, Gaston, and M. Jolas. *The Poetics of Space*. Boston: Beacon, 1994.

Badiou, Alain, and Bruno Bosteels. *Philosophy for Militants*. London: Verso, 2012.

Badiou, Alain, and Gregory Elliott. *The Rebirth of History*. London: Verso, 2012.

Badiou, Alain. *Theory of the Subject*. London: Continuum, 2009.

Badiou, Alain, Wolfgang Schirmacher, and Slavoj Žižek. "On the Truth-Process." An Open Lecture By Alain Badiou. European Graduate School, Saas-Fee. Aug. 2002. *European Graduate School*. Web. 12 June 2013. <http://www.egs.edu/faculty/alain- badiou/articles/on-the-truth-process/>.

Badiou, Alain, Slavoj Žižek, and Peter Engelmann. *Philosophy in the Present*. Cambridge: Polity, 2009.

Badiou, Alain, Fabien Tarby, and Louise Burchill. *Philosophy and the Event.*

Ball, Philip. *Critical Mass: How One Thing Leads to Another*. New York: Farrar, Straus and Giroux, 2004.

Ballard, J. G. *High-rise*. New York: Holt, Rinehart and Winston, 1977.

Baudrillard, Jean. "Contemporary Art: Art Contemporary with Itself." *European Graduate School*. N.p., n.d. Web. 01 Oct. 2013. <http://www.egs.edu/faculty/jean-baudrillard/articles/contemporary-art-art-contemporary-with-itself/>.

---. *Simulacra and Simulation*. Ann Arbor: U of Michigan, 1994.

---. *The System of Objects*. London: Verso, 1996.

Bauman, Zygmunt. *Postmodernity and Its Discontents*. New York: New York University Press, 1997.

Benjamin, Walter, and Rolf Tiedemann. *The Arcades Project*. Cambridge, MA: Belknap, 1999.

Bennington, Geoffrey. "For Better and For Worse (there Again)." *Diactritics* 1-2 38 (2008): 92- 103.

---. *Jacques Derrida*. Chicago: U of Chicago, 1993.

Bensaïd, Daniel. *Marx for Our Times: Adventures and Misadventures of a Critique*. London:Verso, 2002.

Berardi, Franco. *The Uprising: On Poetry and Finance*. Los Angeles: Semiotext(e), 2012.

Borges, Jorge Luis. *El Aleph*. Trans. Norman Thomas Di Giovanni. N.p.: n.p., n.d. N. pag. *MIT Web*. Web. <http://web.mit.edu/allanmc/www/borgesaleph.pdf>.

Boundas, Constantin V. *Deleuze and Philosophy*. Edinburgh: Edinburgh UP, 2006. 297.

Butler, Judith, Ernesto Laclau, and Slavoj Žižek. *Contingency, Hegemony, Universality: Contemporary Dialogues on the Left*. London: Verso, 2010.

Cage, John. For the Birds – John Cage in Conversation with Daniel Charles Boston: M.

Boyars, 1995.

Colebrook, Claire. *Gilles Deleuze*. London: Routledge, 2002.

Coole, Diana H., and Samantha Frost. *New Materialisms: Ontology, Agency, and Politics*. Durham: Duke UP, 2010.

DeLanda, Manuel. *A Thousand Years of Nonlinear History*. New York: Zone, 1997.

---. *Deleuze and the Open-ended Becoming of the World*. Proc. of Chaos/Control: Complexity Conference, Universität Konstanz. 1998. Web. 14 Jan. 2014. <http://www.egs.edu/faculty/manuel-de-landa/articles/deleuze-and-the-open-ended-=becoming-of-the-world/>.

---. *Intensive Science and Virtual Philosophy*. London: Continuum, 2002.

---. *A Thousand Plateaus: Capitalism and Schizophrenia*. London: Continuum, 2004.

---. *Anti-Oedipus: Capitalism and Schizophrenia*. London: Continuum, 2004.

---. *What Is Philosophy?* New York: Columbia UP, 1994.

Deleuze, Gilles. *Difference and Repetition*. New York: Columbia UP, 1994.

---. *Kant's Critical Philosophy: The Doctrine of the Faculties*. London: Continuum, 2008.

---. *The Fold: Leibniz and the Baroque*. Minneapolis: U of Minnesota, 1993.

---. *The Logic of Sense*. New York: Columbia UP, 1990.

---. *Nietzsche and Philosophy*. New York: Columbia UP, 1983.

---. *Proust and Signs*. New York: G. Braziller, 1972

---. *Pure Immanence*. New York: Zone Books, 2000.

Derrida, Jacques, and Maurizio Ferraris. *A Taste for the Secret*. Malden, MA: Polity, 2001.

Derrida, Jacques, and Geoffrey Bennington. *The Beast and the Sovereign*. Chicago: U of Chicago, 2009.

Derrida, Jacques. *The Post Card: From Socrates to Freud and beyond*. Chicago: U of Chicago, 1987.

Derrida, Jacques, and Stefano Agosti. *Spurs: Nietzsche's Styles = Eperons: Les Styles De Nietzsche*. Chicago: U of Chicago, 1979.

Dowd, Garin. *Abstract Machines: Samuel Beckett and Philosophy after Deleuze and Guattari*. Amsterdam: Rodopi, 2007.

Dupuy, Jean Pierre. *Pour Un Catastrophisme Éclairé: Quand L'impossible Est Certain*. Paris: Éditions Du Seuil, 2004.

European Graduate School EGS <http://wwwegs.edu/>.

Feynman, Richard P. *Six Not-so-easy Pieces: Einstein's Relativity, Symmetry, and Space-time*. Reading, MA: Addison-Wesley Pub., 1997.

---. *The Meaning of It All: Thoughts of a Citizen Scientist*. Reading, MA: Addison-Wesley, 1998.

Freud, Sigmund, James Strachey, and Angela Richards. *On Metapsychology: The Theory of Psychoanalysis*. London: Penguin, 1991.

Fynsk, Christopher. Heidegger: Thought and Historicity. Cornell University Press. Ithaca, New York, 1986.

Gaffney, Peter. *The Force of the Virtual: Deleuze, Science, and Philosophy*. Minneapolis: U of Minnesota, 2010.

Hallward, Peter, and Slavoj Žižek. *Badiou: A Subject to Truth*. Minneapolis, MN: U of Minnesota, 2003.

Hallward, Peter. *Out of This World: Deleuze and the Philosophy of Creation*. London: Verso, 2006.

Hardt, Michael. *Gilles Deleuze: An Apprenticeship in Philosophy*. Minneapolis: U of Minnesota, 1993.

Hardt, Michael, and Antonio Negri. "The Fight for 'Real Democracy' at the Heart of Occupy Wall Street." Editorial. *Foreign Affairs* 11 Oct. 2011: n. pag. *European Graduate School*. Web. 02 June 2014. <http://www.egs.edu/faculty/michael-hardt/articles/the-fight-for- real-democracy-at-the-heart-of-occupy-wall-street/>.

Hawking, Stephen. *A Brief History of Time: From the Big Bang to Black Holes*. Toronto: Bantam, 1988.

Hegel, Georg Wilhelm Friedrich, and Stephen Houlgate. *The Hegel Reader*. Oxford, UK: Blackwell, 1998.

Hegel, Georg Wilhelm Friedrich, and J. Sibree. *The Philosophy of History*. New York: Dover Publications, 1956.

Heidegger, Martin, and David Farrell. Krell. *Basic Writings: Martin Heidegger*. London: Routledge, 2010.

Heidegger, Martin. *Being and Time*. New York: Harper, 1962.

---. "Building Dwelling Thinking." *Poetry, Language, Thought*. Trans. Albert Hofstadter. New York: Harper Colophon, 1971. N. pag. *Building Dwelling Thinking*. Web. 11 Mar. 2014. <http://mysite.pratt.edu/~arch543p/readings/Heidegger.html>.

---. Poetry, Language, Thought. Perennial, 2001.

---. *What Is Called Thinking?* Trans. Fred D. Wieck. New York: Harper & Row, 1968.

Heine, Heinrich, and Charles Godfrey Leland. *The Works of Heinrich Heine*. Vol. 14. London: W. Heinemann, 1891.

Hibbert, Christopher. *The French Revolution*. Harmondsworth: Penguin, 1984.

Hobbes, Thomas, and C. B. Macpherson. *Leviathan: Thomas Hobbes; Edited with an Introduction by C. B. Macpherson*. Great Britain: Penguin, 1985.

Inwood, M. J. *A Heidegger Dictionary*. Malden, MA: Blackwell, 2000.

Jameson, Fredric. *Postmodernism, Or, The Cultural Logic of Late Capitalism*. Durham: Duke UP, 1991.

Kant, Immanuel, and Mary J. Gregor. *Practical Philosophy*. Cambridge: Cambridge UP, 1996.

Kant, Immanuel, and Hans Siegbert. Reiss. *Kant: Political Writings*. Cambridge: Cambridge UP, 1991.

Koolhaas, Rem, Stefano Boeri, and Hans Ulrich. Obrist. *Mutations: Rem Koolhaas, Harvard Project on the City, Stefano Boeri, Multiplicity, Sanford Kwinter, Nadia Tazi, Hans Ulrich Obrist*. Barcelona: ACTAR, 2000.

Kouvélakis, Eustache. *Philosophy and Revolution: From Kant to Marx*. London: Verso, 2003.

Kuhn, Thomas S., and Ian Hacking. *The Structure of Scientific Revolutions*. Chicago: U of Chicago, 2012.

Lacan Dot Com. <http://www.lacan.com/>.

Lacan, Jacques, Héloïse Fink, and Bruce Fink. *Ecrits: The First Complete Edition in English*. New York: W.W. Norton, 2006.

Lacan, Jacques. The Four Fundamental Concepts of Psychoanalysis. New York: Norton

Publishers, 1978.

Leach, Neil. *Rethinking Architecture: A Reader in Cultural Theory*. New York: Routledge, 1997.

Lefebvre, Henri. *The Production of Space*. Oxford, OX, UK: Blackwell, 1991.

Lethem, Jonathan. *Dissident Gardens*. New York: Doubleday, 2013.

---. *As She Climbed Across the Table*. Vintage, 1998.

Lindroos, Kia. *Now-time Image-space: Temporalization of Politics in Walter Benjamin's Philosophy of History and Art*. Jyväskylä, Finland: U of Jyväskylä, 1998.

Malabou, Catherine. "The Eternal Return and The Phantom of Difference." Trans. Arne De Boever. *Parrhesia* 10 (2010): 21-29. Web. <http://parrhesiajournal.org/parrhesia10/parrhesia10_malabou.pdf>.

Manning, Erin. *Relationscapes: Movement, Art, Philosophy*. Cambridge, MA: MIT, 2009.

Marx, Karl, Eden Paul, and Cedar Paul. *The Eighteenth Brumaire of Louis Bonaparte*. London: G. Allen & Unwin, 1926.

Massumi, Brian. *A Shock to Thought: Expressions after Deleuze and Guattari*. London: Routledge, 2002.

Matta-Clark, Gordon. Interview by François Vereesen. *Gordon Matta-Clark's Summer 77*. N.p., n.d. Web. 27 Apr. 2014. <http://summer77.eu/applying-liberated-space/>.

Meillassoux, Quentin. "History and Event in Alain Badiou." *Parhessia* 12 (2011): 1-11.

Morton, Brian, and Pamela Collins. *Contemporary Composers*. Chicago: St. James, 1992.

Naas, Michael. *Derrida from Now on*. New York: Fordham UP, 2008.

Nail, Thomas. *Returning to Revolution: Deleuze, Guattari and Zapatismo*. Edinburgh: Edinburgh UP, 2012.

Nancy, Jean-Luc. *Hegel: The Restlessness of the Negative*. Minneapolis, MN: U of Minnesota, 2002.

Nietzsche, Friedrich Wilhelm. *The Gay Science*. Mineola, NY: Dover Publications, 2006.

---. Will To Power. (Trans. Walter Kaufman). New York: Vintage Books, 1967.

A Night at the Opera. Dir. George S. Kaufman, Chico Marx, Groucho Marx, Harpo Marx, and Sam Wood. MGM, n.d. DVD.

Over Your Cities Gras Will Grow. Dir. Sophie Fiennes. Artificial Eye, 2011.

Parrhesia Journal of Critical Philosophy <http://www.parrhesiajournal.org/>.

Parr, Adrian. *The Deleuze Dictionary*. Edinburgh: Edinburgh UP, 2005.

Perec, Georges, and John Sturrock. *Species of Spaces and Other Pieces*. London, England: Penguin, 1997.

The Phaidon Atlas of 21st Century World Architecture. London: Phaidon, 2011.

Rajchman, John. *Constructions*. Cambridge, MA: MIT, 1998.

Ross, Kristin. *May '68 and Its Afterlives*. Chicago: U of Chicago, 2002.

Rubin, Jerry. *Do It; Scenarios of the Revolution*. New York: Simon and Schuster, 1970.

Sample, Ian. *Massive: The Higgs Boson and the Greatest Hunt in Science*. London: Virgin, 2013.

Schirmacher, Wolfgang. "Die Stadt Als Geviert. Fragen Einer Philosophie Der Architektur." *European Graduate School*. N.p., n.d. Web. 17 Mar. 2014. <http://www.egs.edu/faculty/wolfgang-schirmacher/articles/die-stadt-als-Geviert/>.

---. "Homo Generator in the Postmodern Discussion. From a Conversation with Jean-François Lyotard." *European Graduate School*. N.p., n.d. Web. 01 Oct. 2013. <http://www.egs.edu/faculty/wolfgang-schirmacher/articles/homo-generator-in-the-postmodern-discussion/>.

---. "Media as LifeWorld." *Lifeworld and Technology*. Ed. Lester Embree. Washington: n.p., 1989. N. pag. *European Graduate School*. Web. 17 Feb. 2014. <http://www.egs.edu/faculty/wolfgang-schirmacher/articles/media-as-life-world/>.

---. "On the Inability to Recognize the Human Flaw." *Just Living: Philosophy in Artificial Life*. New York: Atropos, n.d. N. pag. *European Graduate School*. Web. 30 Aug. 2013. <http://www.egs.edu/faculty/wolfgang-schirmacher/articles/on-the-inability-to-recognize-the-human-flaw/>.

---. "Technoculture and Life Technique." *European Graduate School*. N.p., n.d. Web. 01 Oct. 2013. <http://www.egs.edu/faculty/wolfgang-schirmacher/articles/technoculture-and-life-technique/>.

---. "The Virtual Human - A Trans Without Qualities." *Anthropologie Der Medien - Mensch Und Kommunikationstechnologien*. N.p.: n.p., 2002. N. pag. *European Graduate School*. Web. 20 Feb. 2014. <http://www.egs.edu/faculty/wolfgang-schirmacher/articles/the-virtual-human/>.

Schrödinger, Erwin. *Space-time Structure*. Cambridge: Cambridge Univ., 1994.

Skakov, Nariman. *The Cinema of Tarkovsky: Labyrinths of Space and Time*. London: I.B. Tauris, 2012.

Smith, Daniel W. *Essays on Deleuze*. Edinburgh: Edinburgh UP, 2012.

Smolin, Lee. *The Trouble with Physics: The Rise of String Theory, the Fall of a Science and What Comes next*. London: Penguin, 2008.

Syndromes and A Century. Dir. Apichatpong Weerasethakul. BFI, 2006.

Williams, James. *Gilles Deleuze's Difference and Repetition: A Critical Introduction and Guide*. Edinburgh: Edinburgh UP, 2003.

Žižek, Slavoj. "Deleuze's Platonism: Ideas as Real." *Lacan.com*. N.p., n.d. Web. 12 Dec. 2013. <http://www.lacan.com/zizplato.htm>.

---. *Event: Philosophy in Transit*. Penguin, Limited, 2014.

---. *Demanding the Impossible*. Malden, MA: Polity, 2013.

---. *First as Tragedy, Then as Farce*. London: Verso, 2009.

---. *How to Read Lacan*. New York: W.W. Norton, 2007.

---. *In Defense of Lost Causes*. London: Verso, 2008.

---. *Less than Nothing: Hegel and the Shadow of Dialectical Materialism*. London: Verso, 2012.

---. *Living in the End times*. London: Verso, 2010.

---. Looking Awry: An Introduction To Lacan Through Popular Culture. Cambridge: The MIT Press, 1992.

---. "Occupy Wall Street: What Is to Be Done Next?" *Theguardian.com*. Guardian News and Media, 24 Apr. 2012. Web. 24 Apr. 2012. <http://www.theguardian.com/commentisfree/cifamerica/2012/apr/24/occupy-wall-street-what-is-to-be-done-next>.

---. *Organs Without Bodies: On Deleuze and Consequences*. Abington, Oxon: Routledge, 2012.

---. *The Parallax View*. Cambridge, MA: MIT, 2006.

---. *The Puppet and the Dwarf: The Perverse Core of Christianity*. Cambridge, MA: MIT, 2003.

---. "Reflections on WTC — Third Version." *Welcome to the Desert of the Real*. London: Verso, 2002. N. pag. *Lacan Dot Com*. Web. 28 June 2011. <http://www.egs.edu/faculty/slavoj-zizek/articles/welcome-to-the-desert-of-the-real/>.

---. *The Sublime Object of Ideology*. London: Verso, 1989.

---. *Tarrying with the Negative: Kant, Hegel, and the Critique of Ideology*. Durham: Duke UP, 1993.

---. *The Year of Dreaming Dangerously*. London: Verso, 2012.

Žižek, Slavoj, Rex Butler, and Scott Stephens. *Interrogating the Real*. London: Continuum, 2006.

Žižek, Slavoj, Elizabeth Wright, and Edmond Leo Wright. *The Žižek Reader*. Oxford, UK: Blackwell, 1999.

Think Media: EGS Media Philosophy Series

Wolfgang Schirmacher, *editor*

A Postcognitive Negation: The Sadomasochistic Dialectic of American Psychology, Matthew Giobbi
A World Without Reason, Jeff McGary
All for Nothing, Rachel K. Ward
Asking, for Telling, by Doing, as if Betraying, Stephen David Ross
Memory and Catastrophe, Joan Grossman
Can Computers Create Art?, James Morris
Community without Identity: The Ontology and Politics of Heidegger, Tony See
Deleuze and the Sign, Christopher M. Drohan
Deleuze: History and Science, Manuel DeLanda
DRUGS Rhetoric of Fantasy, Addiction to Truth, Dennis Schep
Facticity, Poverty and Clones: On Kazuo Ishiguro's 'Never Let Me Go', Brian Willems
Fear and Laughter: A Politics of Not Selves 'For' Self, Jake Reeder
Gratitude for Technology, Baruch Gottlieb
Hospitality in the Age of Media Representation, Christian Hänggi
Itself, Robert Craig Baum
Jack Spicer: The Poet as Crystal Radio Set, Matthew Keenan
Laughter and Mourning: point of rupture, Pamela Noensie
Letters to a Young Therapist: Relational Practices for the Coming Community, Vincenzo Di Nicola
Literature as Pure Mediality: Kafka and the Scene of Writing, Paul DeNicola
Media Courage: ImpossiblePedagogy in an Artificial Community, Fred Isseks
Metastaesthetics, Nicholas Alexander Hayes
Mirrors triptych technology: Remediation and Translation Figures, Diana Silberman Keller
Necessity of Terrorism political evolution and assimilation, Sharif Abdunnur
No Future Now, Denah Johnston
Nomad X, Drew Minh
On Becoming-Music: Between Boredom and Ecstasy, Peter Price
Painting as Metaphor, Sarah Nind
Performing the Archive: The Transformation of the Archive in Contemporary Art from Repository of Documents to Art Medium, Simone Osthoff
Philosophy of Media Sounds, Michael Schmidt
Polyrhythmic Ethics, Julia Tell
Propaganda of the Dead: Terrorism and Revolution, Mark Reilly
Repetition, Ambivalence and Inarticulateness: Mourning and Memory in Western Heroism, Serena Hashimoto
Resonance: Philosophy for Sonic Art, Peter Price

Schriftzeichen der Wahrheit: Zur Philosophie der Filmsprache, Alexander J. Klemm
Scratch & Sniff, Peter van de Kamp
Shamanism + Cyberspace, Mina Cheon
Sonic Soma: Sound, Body and the Origins of the Alphabet, Elise Kermani
Sovereignty in Singularity: Aporias in Ethics and Aesthetics, Gregory Bray
The Art of the Transpersonal Self: Transformation as Aesthetic and Energetic Practice, Norbert Koppensteiner
The Ethics of Uncertainty: Aporetic Openings, Michael Anker
The Image That Doesn't Want to be Seen, Kenneth Feinstein
The Infinite City: Politics of Speed, Asli Telli Aydemir
The Media Poet, Michelle Cartier
The Novel Imagery: Aesthetic Response as Feral Laboratory, Dawan Stanford
The Organic Organisation: freedom, creativity and the search for fulfilment, Nicholas Ind
The Suicide Bomber; and her gift of death, Jeremy Fernando
The Transreal Political Aesthetics of Crossing Realities, Micha Cárdenas
Theodore, Sofia Fasos
Trans Desire/Affective Cyborgs, Micha Cárdenas
Trans/actions: art, film and death, Bruce Barber
Transience: A poiesis, of dis/appearance, Julia Hölzl
Trauma, Hysteria, Philosophy, Hannes Charen
Upward Crashes Fracture's Topoi: Musil, Kiefer, Darger, Paola Piglia-Veronese

Other books available from Atropos Press

5 Milton Stories (For the Witty, Wise and Worldly Child), Sofia Fasos Korahais
Che Guevara and the Economic Debate in Cuba, Luiz Bernardo Pericás
Grey Ecology, Paul Virilio
heart, speech, this, Gina Rae Foster
Follow Us or Die, Vincent W.J., van Gerven Oei
Just Living: Philosophy in Artificial Life. Collected Works Volume 1, Wolfgang Schirmacher
Laughter, Henri Bergson
Pessoa, The Meaphysical Courier, Judith Balso
Philosophical Essays: from Ancient Creed to Technological Man, Hans Jonas
Philosophy of Culture, Schopenhauer and Tradition, Wolfgang Schirmacher
Talking Cheddo: Teaching Hard Kushitic Truths Liberating PanAfrikanism, Menkowra Manga Clem Marshall
Teletheory, Gregory L. Ulmer
The Tupperware Blitzkrieg, Anthony Metivier
Vilém Flusser's Brazilian Vampyroteuthis Infernalis, Vilém Flusser

www.ingramcontent.com/pod-product-compliance
Lightning Source LLC
LaVergne TN
LVHW010102110826
845155LV00028B/454

* 9 7 8 1 9 4 0 8 1 3 2 2 6 *